1

MARXIFICATION OF EDUCATION

OF

THE
MARXIFICATION
OF
EDUCATION

Paulo Freire's Critical Marxism and the Theft of Education

JAMES LINDSAY, PhD
PRESIDENT AND FOUNDER OF NEW DISCOURSES
newdiscourses.com

 New Discourses

Copyright © 2022 by James Lindsay

All rights reserved. No part of this book may be reproduced in any form by an
electronic or mechanical means, including information storage and retrieval
systems, without permission in writing from the publisher.

First edition: December 2022

Cover copyright © 2022 New Discourses, LLC.

Paperback ISBN: 9798355360108
Hardcover ISBN: 9798355360269

Imprint: Independently published

Published by New Discourses, LLC.
Orlando, Florida
https://newdiscourses.com

For Tiffany and Tina and all the moms
fighting for liberty for our children

CONTENTS

PROLOGUE

In the wake of the horrific school shooting at Robb Elementary School in Uvalde, Texas, on May 24, 2022, people across the nation were grasping through their shock and horror for answers and for solutions. Little is more terrifying than a school shooting. Little, also, is more divisive.

Predictably, everything split along party lines in the wake of the tragedy, which meant Democrats pushed as vigorously as ever for gun control while Republicans defended the value and necessity of the Second Amendment. Many parents, easily the constituency most shaken and in need of answers and workable solutions to keep their children safe in schools, were caught in the middle.

Indicative of this kind of political posturing, just two days later, on May 26, Democratic State Senator Tiara Mack ("she/her") of Rhode Island, who bills herself as a "queer educator," "donut lover," and "abortion fundraiser" on her Twitter profile and who later became (in)famous for a viral self-promotional "campaign" video of her standing on her head in a bikini and twerking upside-down, tweeted a picture of a hundred or two children and teens lying on the ground at the Rhode Island Statehouse with the following caption:

> Students from a few Providence schools walked out today and laid down for 3 min [sic] outside the RI State House [sic]. Will we pass common sense [sic] gun legislation this session in RI?[1]

---

1   https://twitter.com/MackDistrict6/status/1529869073873510400

Typical political profiteering, sure, a bit classless, one might think, and think no more, but there's important context lurking behind this political stunt. Erika Sanzi, outreach coordinator for Parents Defending Education, pointed out a glaring elephant in the educational room soon thereafter, also on Twitter, in a broadcast response to Mack's tweet.

> 94% of Providence students aren't proficient in math.
> 86% can't read or write on grade level.
> Legislators who never talk about student outcomes proudly use students during school hours as foot soldiers for their activism.[2]

Haunting the scene of the activist stunt promoted by Mack—no doubt organized and facilitated by activist teachers—there's a story of abysmal academic failure in Providence schools. Children in Rhode Island seem to be learning almost nothing except that when something big happens in the news, it's time to pull a performative political stunt in order to attempt to get one's political way, nearly always for left-wing causes.

What's going on here? Parents deserve to know. Our children deserve far better than this. Our nation and its future depend on correcting it. Well, there's actually a simple answer. The overwhelmingly primary reason 94% of Providence students are failing mathematics and 86% cannot read or write at grade level but can turn out by the hundreds to a left-wing political demonstration at the Rhode Island Statehouse during school hours is unambiguous once understood: education has been stolen right out from under us and from our children. This theft of education has a purpose; it enables a counterfeit to replace it. The mechanism and description of this gigantic educational ripoff can be summarized in a single sentence: *Our kids go to Paulo Freire's schools.*

---

2   https://twitter.com/esanzi/status/1529968989413249025

Chances are that unless you're a Brazilian, an educator, or deep into the front lines of the battles in the culture war, or a happy listener to my podcasts, you have never heard of Paulo Freire and have no idea what this means. Well, you need to. Paulo Freire is easily the most influential name in education in a century, and as a result, as I said, *our kids go to Paulo Freire's schools.* Almost all of them do. In this guidebook, I hope to introduce you sufficiently to Paulo Freire's theory of education, which dominates all colleges of education in North America today along with most K–12 schools, to help you understand why, when I saw the two tweets quoted above, I immediately knew what was going on. The schools in Providence, Rhode Island, are Paulo Freire's schools, and Marxist activists posing as teachers and politicians are coordinating to take advantage of the output of that fact to stage a huge political demonstration using Providence children as happy and willing props. In turn, these children are being "conscientized" as activists for causes useful to Marxist political agenda items.

As you will see, these students were participating not only in activism, as demanded by Freirean education, but they were also learning to "decodify" the alleged deeper political circumstances of a school shooting. That is, they were learning to adopt the political framing of the activists posing as their teachers and state representatives. The tragedy in Uvalde was being falsely presented to them as a "codification" of the "actual" political circumstances of *their own lives* in the United States and Rhode Island in 2022. They were learning Freirean "political literacy" even while their schools fail them almost completely in actual literacy. This is by design in a Freirean school, despite palatable marketing to the contrary.

The overwhelming adoption of Paulo Freire's crackpot theory of education, which has become known as "Critical Pedagogy," may relate to but cannot *directly* explain the rise in school shootings, inexplicable failures of law enforcement, or many other tragedies. It does, however, *almost completely* explain why our schools are failing to teach our children basic skills like reading, writing, and mathematics while succeeding at turning them into a new activist class for Leftist—and *only* and *explicitly* Leftist—causes. This is what Freire's educational theory is designed to achieve. Students are meant to be "facilitated" into Leftist political activism, and other student achievement outcomes are quite literally an afterthought. Education is a pretext; Marxist activist grooming is the point.

The catastrophe of Freirean education is difficult to overstate. In fact, it's best stated by Freirean educators themselves, as they attempt to salvage the disastrous method from its own programmatic failure. Consider the following description from the German adult education institute DVV International (*Deutscher Volkshochschul-Verband*), which attempted to study the implementation of Freirean pedagogy in the Nigerian context in 2007.

Stage Two: The Selection of Words from The Discovered Vocabulary
From the discussions of the learners, the Generative Words written by the team of facilitators were: resources, money, abundance, crude oil, stealing, pocket, begging, plenty, poverty, suffering, frustration, crying, hunger, crisis, dying, death.

These words were later depicted in pictorial form showing the concrete realities and situations in the lives of the people. The pictorial display provoked an emotional state of pity and anger among the discussants, some of them could not talk, while most of them were moved to tears asking the question: Why! Why! Why! Why!

Stage Three: The Actual Process of Literacy Training
After the completion of stage two, it came as a great surprise to the facilitators, that the discussants were not willing to participate in the literacy teaching/training process. They were in a state of emotional wreck. They were furious, angry, shouting and restless. They were shouting Change! Change! Change! Cursing furiously those who have,

in one way or the other, contributed to the suffering of the people. The bottom-line: acquisition of basic literacy skills did not make any meaning to them and in fact was irrelevant, with some of them asking the facilitators:

"What have you people, who are learned, done to change the situation, rather you (have) worsened the situation when you yourself get to the position."[3]

As in Nigeria, so in Rhode Island—and anywhere else Freirean pedagogy is used to steal education. Freirean pedagogy is a cult indoctrination, though, and its purveyors are its cultists. It cannot be wrong. This is why the conclusion to this paper, documenting the obvious disaster of the Freirean approach, recommends applying it, though more cautiously, in literacy programs in the future. It shall not be abandoned. Why? The method doesn't fail at its primary objective, whatever it does with its stated objective, which is little more than its sales pitch. The method very successfully and efficiently achieves political conscientization; of that there can be no doubt.

The problem, to Freirean educators, is superficial, then. It is only that political conscientization may inadvertently radicalize learners so effectively that they not only fail to learn to read—the nominal justification for the method in the first place—but fail to see the point in learning to read at all. The method must be kept, no matter how disastrous or predictable the disaster, but so must the attempted justification.

As important as the first two stages of Freirean literacy

---

3   Ojokheta, K.O. "Paulo Freire's Literacy Teaching Methodology: Application and Implications of the Methodology in Basic Literacy Classes in Ibadan, Oyo State, Nigeria." Education for Everyone. Worldwide. Lifelong. / Adult Education and Development / Editions / AED 69/2007. https://www. dvv-international.de/en/adult-education-and-development/editions/aed-692007/10th-anniversary-of-paulo-freirersquos-death/paulo-freirersquos-literacy-teaching-methodology

methodology are, facilitators must exercise caution in their application in literacy classes. When the political consciousness of the learners is raised, they may not be patient enough or be interested in the acquisition of literacy skills since the first two stages may have thoroughly conscientized and sensitized them to the realities of their lives. This is the major finding of the study.[4]

This guide exists to make the case, supported by Freire's own words, that the researchers behind this study are the ones who have missed the point. Learning to read (or achieve academically in any subject) has always been little more than a palatable cover for Freire's actual objective: raising Marxist political consciousness for the purposes of creating a cultural revolution. Consider the following three remarks from Freire in his significant 1985 book *The Politics of Education: Culture, Power, and Liberation*. The first of these is slightly technical but should be comprehensible enough with a little explanation.

> *Codification*: the imaging of a significant aspect of a man's existential situation in a slum [given as an example of a context in which he lives]. The generative word ["slum"] is inserted in this codification [as the educational subject matter presented to the student]. The codification functions as the knowable object mediating between the knowing subjects—the educator and learners—in the act of knowing they achieve in dialogue (*The Politics of Education*, p. 91)

What needs to be drawn out from this sample of Freire's text is a theme that occurs over and over again throughout his books: the lesson presented by the educator *is a mediator of learning*. It is not something to be learned in and of itself; it is something that facilitates learning on the terms Freire is setting. In other words, a math lesson isn't just a math lesson anymore. It's a mediator to another kind of lesson, which for Freire is a *political* (read: Marxist) lesson. The math lesson, or any

---

4   *Ibid.*

other lesson, merely becomes the vehicle to the political conversation Freire thinks constitutes real education.

> From the linguistic point of view, if an illiterate is one who does not know how to read and write, a political illiterate—regardless of whether she or he knows how to read and write—is one who has an ingenuous perception of humanity in its relationships with the world. This person has a naive outlook on social reality, which for this one is a given, that is, social reality is a *fait accompli* rather than something that's still in the making. (p. 103)

For Freire, *political* literacy clearly matters, not just actual illiteracy. Indeed, as we will see, actual literacy is, at best, a secondary concern. He feels this way because, in keeping with Karl Marx, whose theology he adopted in full, man's true nature lies in gaining the power to transform the world (into a socialist utopia through relentless critique of what *is*), and his ability to participate in this process of political activism and transformation is the most fundamental aspect of his being and his key human right.

> As an event calling forth the critical reflection of both the learners and educators, the literacy process must relate *speaking the word* to *transforming reality*, and to man's role in this transformation. Perceiving the significance of that relationship is indispensable for those learning to read and write if we are really committed to liberation. Such a perception will lead the learners to recognize a much greater right than that of being literate. They will ultimately recognize that, as men, they have the right to have a voice. (p. 51)

"Why! Why! Why! Why! Change! Change! Change!" the Nigerian "learners" shouted as they wailed, gnashed their teeth, and vigorously rejected their literacy lessons after gaining "political literacy" and being "conscientized and sensitized" to "the realities of their lives," but this isn't just half a world away in West Africa sometime in the past. It isn't hard to imagine hearing the same from the largely functionally illiterate and innumerate "emotionally wrecked" children and teenagers lying on the steps of the Rhode Island statehouse in Providence this year, cheered on and driven by a radical Leftist in the state senate. "Why! Why! Why! Why! Change! Change! Change!" The reason is simple: *our kids go to Paulo Freire's schools.* Speaking for change is a "much greater right than that of being literate," so "acquisition of basic literacy skills did not make any meaning to them and in fact was irrelevant." The result is the same because the process is the same, and, for its intended purpose—but not its stated purpose—the process *works.*

This has to stop. It never should have been allowed to happen. This is not what education should be about, and it cannot be what education is about in any nation that hopes to survive long into the future. In fact, it isn't education at all. It is, in a phrase, *thought reform,* which Robert Jay Lifton gave as the formal translation for the Mandarin Chinese *xǐnǎo* (洗 脑), which literally translates as "wash brain," or, more commonly, *brainwashing.* Another apt term in our more contemporary context is (cult) *grooming.*

By the end of this guide, chances are good that you'll understand the biggest piece of why our schools are failing kids and turning them into self-defeating, ignorant, often paranoid activists for causes they don't even understand, and you'll probably agree with me—unless you're a certain type of Marxist yourself. Paulo Freire's influence needs to be identified and removed from every school and college of education in North America and throughout the world as quickly as possible for the sake of our families, our nations, and, most of all, our kids.

James Lindsay
August 2022

I. Introduction:

THE THEFT OF EDUCATION

Much of the theory and practice of education (pedagogy) employed today in North American schools is derived directly, with certain contextual updates and modifications, from the work of a Brazilian Marxist radical by the name of Paulo Freire. While Freire isn't exactly a household name in the United States, he is a household name and figure of educational legend in *all* North American colleges of education. So is his approach, which is called "Critical Pedagogy" or "Critical Education Theory." In colleges of education throughout North America, in fact, Freire is revered, and his work is considered virtually sacrosanct. It has accordingly been incredibly influential. Because of his incredible sway in North American colleges of education, Paulo Freire is recognized as the third most-cited scholarly author in all of the humanities and social sciences by authoritative metrics. It exaggerates none at all to state that Paulo Freire is at the theoretical center of everything happening in colleges of education today, and from there our nations' schools. A succinct way to phrase the consequences of his influence on education is that *our kids go to Paulo Freire's schools*.

What this means is nothing short of *the theft of education*. Something that looks like education remains, but it is no longer education. It is political brainwashing to see the world "on the side of the oppressed." So central to his views is this transformation of education that Freire's *magnum opus* bears the description of it in the title: it is the *Pedagogy of the Oppressed*, in which educators and learners together are instructed to "die and be resurrected" on the side of the oppressed and into a "faith" in "permanent struggle." Students are transformed into learners who learn virtually nothing except two things: (1) how to view the world from the "standpoint of the oppressed," and (2) to denounce the "dehumanizing conditions" of the world, as seen from that perspective, in a way that simultaneously announces the potential for something "better" (read: more Socialist, equitable, and Socially Just).

The mechanism for this theft of education was straightforward and generational: capture and transform the colleges of education; mold a generation of teachers; program every generation of students thereafter. Colleges of education were captured almost entirely to the Freirean approach by no later than 1995, and the intervening quarter century has seen enough turnover of the teachers to have fundamentally remade our schools and thus education itself. Kids still go to school, but school isn't school anymore. The teachers have been replaced with activists, and education has been turned into "conscientization," the process of seeing the world from the so-called standpoint of the oppressed.

Many of the major seemingly faddish but broadly dominant developments in education today have roots that can be traced back in whole or in part to Paulo Freire. These include, especially, the abysmal performance in achieving at-grade-level competency in most subjects in most classes in most schools, misplaced curricular emphases, the rampant data-mining of children through relentless surveys and assessments (though these serve other purposes as well), Culturally Relevant (and Responsive) Teaching, "decolonizing" the curriculum, student-led project-based learning, and Social-Emotional Learning (SEL), especially "Transformative" Social-Emotional Learning. Other programs, like Comprehensive Sexuality Education (CSE)—including the abominable practice of Drag Queen Story Hour, in which drag queens (adult men dressed as clown-form sexualized women) do drag performances for children while reading to them in school libraries and classrooms—graft themselves onto the Freirean "generative" method. It is because of this methodological approach that they are able to do what they do and to justify their inclusion in (early) childhood education.

Some of these trends are direct and intended consequences of Freirean pedagogy. These include focusing on social issues through broadly Marxian social theories like Critical Race Theory, the "democratic" (that is, ungovernable) classroom, and the grooming of children into "critically conscious" activist "change agents." These are the reasons Freirean pedagogy was developed in the first place.

Other trends are an indirect but *not necessarily unintended* result of applying Freire's pedagogy. For example, Freire's approach does not *directly* intend to cause the readily observed widespread underperformance of students across virtually every grade level in virtually every core academic competency (reading, writing, mathematics, scientific literacy, historical literacy, and civics, in particular), but it contributes significantly to it. Part of this failure probably isn't intended. Freire claims his program is about literacy, and yet this failing result is reliable from his method. This is because Freire's method simply gets education wrong, misprioritizes the classroom and educational purpose, and disengages students from academic learning objectives in favor of political activism. On the other hand, part of this result probably *is* intended, since Freire indicts all other models of education as leading to the reproduction of the society he wants to see overthrown in cultural revolution. That is, Freire doesn't want education that teaches people how to be successful in a society he wants to see cast down.

Still others of these trends, like Culturally Relevant Teaching, are little more than a direct and cheap repackaging of Freirean education into a more contemporary identity-political (or "Woke") domain. Yet further others draw upon or are direct consequences of

Freire's pedagogy as it is put into application, even including Social-Emotional Learning, which otherwise has a distinct pedagogical genealogy (or two) but has been explicitly Freirean in approach for at least a decade, if not reaching back to its formal establishment out of "whole-child education" in 1994. Still even further others, like Comprehensive Sexuality Education, don't have obvious *roots* in Freire's work themselves but insinuate themselves into schooling and advance their agenda specifically by using the Freirean framework. (Some others, like the attention given to the practice of educational "scaffolding" are not attributable to Freirean pedagogy. Scaffolding derives more or less directly from the ideas of another controversial and influential name in education, Lev Vygotsky, and his vague notion of the "Zone of Proximal Development." This idea, ZPD, contributes to the project-based learning environment and peer-teaching models, however, onto which Freirean-derived "democratic classrooms" connect efficiently in those domains.)

Understanding the unfolding catastrophe in our schools today—both public and private—is therefore a matter of understanding Paulo Freire and his work. His approach enabled long-marching Communists to steal education from us. Though a thoroughgoing biography is not necessary, some understanding of his thought and approach are needed.

Paulo Freire and the Transformation of Education

Paulo Freire was not merely an educator. He was a postcolonialist radical and a Marxist. He must also be understood as a religious figure, specifically a Liberation Theologian, or at least a devotee to Liberation Theology, which is best summarized by saying it is Marxism pretending to be Catholicism. The religious notes of Freire's pedagogy—in the theology of Marxism—are not merely incidental and do not just run as a current in the background. They are utterly central to his work, which therefore must be recognized as a form of explicitly and intentionally religious instruction. As a matter of fact, it would be best to regard Paulo Freire as the chief revivalist for the theology and practice of Marxism in the last half of the twentieth century. In the end, the simplest summary of Paulo Freire's extensive body of work is that he *Marxified* education and, in turn, made it into a form of religious instruction that our state currently fully endorses, funds, supports, promotes, and demands.

To say Freire "Marxified" education isn't to say that Freire injected Marxist ideas into education, and it is also not to say that Freire adapted education into a form of Marxist indoctrination, as we'd usually understand it. Freire changed the theory of education (pedagogy) itself into a Marxist theory of pedagogy. He even changed what it means to be educated (or literate) at all in the same way. Freire created a Marxist Theory of *knowing* that runs beneath his entire theory of education, and he built a Marxist praxis of thought reform around it. That is his legacy.

His schools—which virtually all of our children in North America attend, at least to some degree—therefore treat education as a Marxist would treat education if *knowing itself* was understood as a kind of cultural capital Marx, if he saw it that way, would call to abolish. This, in my opinion, is the chief reason American schools are failing so completely at teaching children to read, write, do mathematics, understand history and civics, and become scientifically literate, even at grade level, despite substantial and ever-increasing public and other resources being dedicated to the task of education. The purpose of what Freirean schools consider "education" isn't *any* of that. Instead, it's making Marxists out of your children.

Throughout the United States, the failure of academic achievement in public schools in particular is utterly condemning, even by somewhat paltry standards as considered internationally. Though it varies by subject, grade level, and state, at-grade-level academic achievement in U.S. public schools is often well below half of students and is often below a third of them. Illiteracy and innumeracy are increasingly the expectation, not a deviation from it, to be dealt with through increasing demands for programs, money, and "equity," another Marxist end. None of these will succeed so long as Freirean pedagogy stays at the heart of education. Setting the money on fire would be a better use of it (as would letting people keep it!).

Meanwhile, classrooms get less and less governable thanks to related (Marxist) trends like "Restorative Justice," and students are increasingly alienated from the schooling process and the academic content in their schools (by both programs). This unconscionable failure is taking place against a backdrop of apparently increasingly rigorous standards and evaluation (Common Core, Every Student Succeeds Act, etc.), rampant involvement and grant-giving from now-suspicious foundations[5] and NGOs,[6] and a river of additional state and federal moneys pouring into schools—often illegitimately purposed, including through the CARES Act, which appropriates pandemic-relief funding. Many factors contribute to the failure of education in this regard, but little is said directly about the enormous impact of Paulo Freire's disastrous ideas, which cannot lead to academic success no matter how much money is dumped into pushing them. In fact, we have every reason to believe that the better these approaches are funded, the *worse* educational outcomes can be expected to be.

The Great Heist of North American Education
This is because Paulo Freire's Critical Pedagogy is an abject *anti-educational failure* that should be ripped out of our Pre-K–12 schools and

---

5   Including the Bill and Melinda Gates Foundation, the Rockefeller Foundation, the Open Society Foundation, the Fetzer Institute, and many others.
6   Notably including the OECD (Organization for Economic Cooperation and Development), UNESCO (United Nations Educational, Scientific, and Cultural Organization), and the World Bank, coordinated and encouraged through the World Economic Forum.

colleges of education as soon and as thoroughly as possible. Indeed, it never should have been adopted in the first place, and the people who saw to it that it was should be held accountable for the unbelievable damage it has caused in the intervening *forty years*. These ideas were terrible and unfounded when they were written down in the 1960s and when they were accepted in North America in the 1980s, and they haven't improved one iota in the intervening decades. Their adoption and inclusion in North American colleges of education first, and primary and secondary schools second, should be considered one of the greatest academic scandals in the history of the world. Indeed, the "Critical" theft of education should be considered nothing short of a crime against humanity.

The fact that Freire cites or references virtually *no* educational scholarship but bases his work directly upon the likes of Karl Marx, Vladimir Lenin, Che Guevara, Fidel Castro, Rosa Luxemburg, Ivan Illich, Dom Hélder Câmara, Herbert Marcuse, Erich Fromm, and Georg Wilhelm Friedrich Hegel should have been disqualifying enough to prevent the widespread adoption of his work. Instead, it was taken as proof of the need for a radical overhaul of all of educational theory and practice. (Incidentally, or perhaps ironically, the quasi-Marxist school reformers in the "social reform" movement that preceded Critical Pedagogy—Dewey, Counts, Vygotsky—may be responsible for much of the apparent need to overhaul a failing educational methodology.) The scope of the scandal and what it stole from our societies is so incredible as to be difficult to communicate.

Nevertheless, thanks to the relentless efforts ("praxis") of Critical Marxist educators, most of all his disciple and evangelist Henry Giroux, who is openly a Communist, Freire's work was eventually welcomed into the heart of the North American academic educational canon. This occurred significantly because of the tireless work of Giroux and other Critical Pedagogues in the 1970s and 1980s. Giroux deserves the most blame for this unlikely feat, however, since he personally worked through the first half of the 1980s to see that at least one hundred Critical Marxists were tenured as professors in colleges of education. Thus, by the time Paulo Freire's 1985 book *The Politics of Education* burst onto the North American scene following a favorable review in the *Harvard Educational Review* in that same year, the Critical Pedagogy runway was laid, and the plane carrying this failure of an educational model could land in the North American education scene.

This Girouxian praxis was, in turn, facilitated by the relentless work of countless Critical Marxists—including many former members of the radical terrorist organization called the Weather Underground. These "sixties radicals," in the wake of the failures of the neo-Marxist revolutions of the late 1960s, turned away from radical direct activism and made their way into K–12 education activism and the universities, especially the colleges of education. Iowa State University Critical Pedagogue Isaac Gottesman documents this shift in the opening paragraph of his 2016 book, *The Critical Turn in Education*, which chronicles the Woke Marxification of education from the 1970s to the present.

> "To the question: 'Where did all the sixties radicals go?', the most accurate answer," noted Paul Buhle (1991) in his classic *Marxism in the United States*, "would be: neither to religious cults nor yuppiedom, but to the classroom" (p. 263). After the fall of the New Left arose a new left, an Academic Left. For many of these young scholars, Marxist thought, and particularly what some refer to as Western Marxism or neo-Marxism, and what I will refer to as the critical Marxist tradition, was an intellectual anchor. As participants in the radical politics of the sixties entered graduate school and moved into faculty positions and started publishing, the critical turn began to change scholarship throughout the humanities and social sciences. The field of education was no exception. (p. 1)

This shift out of the streets and into the classroom occurred at least in part following the strategic advice of the most significant Critical Marxist of the 1960s and 1970s, Herbert Marcuse. He indicated it was the most fruitful direction for achieving an eventual revolution via the "long march through the institutions" in his desperate 1972 book, *Counter-revolution and Revolt*. He puts it this way,

> To extend the base of the student movement, Rudi Dutschke has proposed the strategy of the *long march through the institutions*: working against the established institutions while working in them, but not simply by "boring from within," rather by "doing the job," learning how to program and read computers, how to teach at all levels of education, how to use the mass media, how to organize production, how to recognize and eschew planned obsolescence, how to design, et cetera), and at the same time preserving one's own consciousness in working with the others. (p. 55)

This infiltration of the educational sphere—*at all levels*—Marcuse says should run along in parallel to establishing a Leftist media, and these objectives therefore depend heavily upon turning education. He's quite explicit about this plan.

> I have stressed the key role which the universities play in the present period: they can still function as institutions for the training of counter-cadres. The "restructuring" necessary for the attainment of this goal means more than decisive student participation and non-authoritarian learning. Making the university "relevant" for today and tomorrow means, instead, presenting the facts and forces that made civilization what it is today and what it could be tomorrow— and that is political education. For history indeed repeats itself; it is this repetition of domination and submission that must be halted,

and halting it presupposes knowledge of its genesis and of the ways in which it is reproduced: critical thinking. (p. 56)

Freire devotes an entire chapter in *The Politics of Education* to "the process of political literacy," which he places as the center of the purpose of education. As such, much of Freire's work can be understood as a profound current within this neo-Marxist course of thought and activism: a project to take over *everything* from within by getting inside of it, "doing the job," and bringing consciousness into the new role. Put otherwise, by two women's studies professors from Arizona State University, Breanne Fahs and Michael Karger, education should be turned into a vehicle for "viral" replication of the ideology, which can then go on to "infect" other domains of life by going with the reprogrammed students out into the world. That is, just as viruses hijack and steal a cell's machinery to make more viruses, this vision hijacks and steals education to create activists and ideologues who will go out into the professional world to infect disciplines, institutions, and industries with Marxism.

As with Marcuse, education, for Freire, must be political education. Education can therefore either teach students to reproduce the existing system or to become "change agents" to "liberate" humanity from it. In that regard, Paulo Freire is among the most significant links between the dying embers of Critical Marxism in the mid-20th century and the Woke Marxist revolution that has captured the world in the second and third decades of the 21st century. He is the Great Revivalist for the faith of Marxism.

It is in this sense—that education can either reproduce the existing system or create the conditions for its demise in (Marxist) revolution—that Freire "Marxified" education, at least on the surface. Education is immediately split by this dirty trick into two. The existing education is framed as false, ideological, if not chauvinist (or bigoted), and the Marxist education program becomes the only possibility for freedom. This moralizing false choice is the basis for the entirety of the Freirean educational fraud that follows and enables the total theft of education from its primary beneficiaries and stakeholders: society, parents, and our kids.

In the coming sections, we will explore more of who Paulo Freire is, how he Marxified education, and what this means. After that, we will devote several sections to the key operational programs within Freirean education. By the end of this guide, Freirean thought reform will be plainly visible to anyone looking at North American educational contexts and understood as the Marxist manipulation (of our children) that it is.

II.
WHO WAS PAULO FREIRE?

As mentioned previously, an extensive biography of Paulo Freire and a thorough documentation of the havoc he wreaked upon Brazilian education is not necessary here, though some details will flesh out our understanding of his method. Throughout his published works, most importantly his two most famous books, *The Pedagogy of the Oppressed* (1970) and *The Politics of Education* (1985), he reveals enough of his character through the names he repeatedly invokes: Karl Marx, G.W.F. Hegel, Vladimir Lenin, Mao Zedong, Fidel Castro, and, in pride of place, Che Guevara. Few, if any, theorists of education (pedagogues) are ever named, referenced, or put into application.

Why would they be? Other educational theories, as we just saw, would fail by Freirean standards because, to the degree that they work to educate students, they lead students to learn to reproduce the existing "oppressive" system. Freire does not want this system reproduced. Freire's followers, like Henry Giroux, implemented his system specifically as the solution to what mid-century Marxists in the twentieth century called "the problem of reproduction," by which the institutions of society, especially education, seemingly intrinsically reproduce the society they operate within. They therefore follow Freire into his "Utopian hope" based upon ruthlessly and relentlessly criticizing all that exists. In the faith bearing that hope, Freire calls *repeatedly*, dozens upon dozens of times, for an outright *and perpetual* cultural revolution by which all "dehumanizing structures" will be thrown down in a perpetual cycle of destruction. This society will be cast down, as will the society that replaces it, and the society that replaces that, and so on and so forth... until Utopia.

Freire, therefore, instead of building upon educational theory, steps upon a soapbox, denounces it all, and declares a Marxist Theory of education—while speaking generously of the most notorious Marxist figures in the broader Communist movements of the 20th century. Learners in this process are meant, in his own words, to be educated so that they can learn to "speak the word in order to proclaim the world." (Christian readers are invited to shudder as this is literally the role uniquely assigned to God in the Bible, and learning to do so as men would be tantamount to acquiring the *gnosis* that we can be as gods.) That world is the Critical Marxist Utopia at the End of History.

Paulo Freire, Postcolonialist Radical

To understand more of how Freire came to be this misguided about the purpose of education, we, perhaps ironically, need to understand Freire's context. Due to political turmoil in Brazil, Freire's middle-class family was badly dispossessed in his youth, plunging them into extreme and devastating poverty. The scars this injustice left upon Freire obviously shaped his views about society and colonialism in Latin America in a profound way. In fact, the experience led him to take up with a considerable amount of radical (and Marxist-influenced) postcolonialist activism and thought, a bent toward (Marxist) liberationism, and a feeling of (Marxist) solidarity with the poor of the Third World. He was particularly aggrieved at colonialist outreach programs, wanting to inspire the peasants of Brazil to rise up on their own terms and take their lives back.

Already deeply seated in this aggrieved mood, Freire began his work in education in the context of adult literacy education in Third World colonized nations in the 1950s and early 1960s in Brazil. In that regard, he was a radical postcolonialist in the mold of the Algerian Frantz Fanon, who advocated violence as a means of recovering one's sense of self from the colonized state. This radical postcolonialism therefore saw the only remedy to colonialism as a complete throwing-off of the colonizing culture to restore that which was there—at the root—before colonization occurred. In these Third World contexts unsullied by colonization, postcolonialists imagine a more idyllic past before colonialism (and Marxists maintain the same fantasy about industrialization). Industrialization swept in with alien colonizers, intimates Freire, and deposed the farmers, who were until that point at the centers of their communities, by changing society, moving them from center out to margin. This, Freire describes explicitly as an act of violence.

> Still more, the structural perception of illiteracy revealed in these texts exposes the other false view of illiterates as marginal men. Those who consider them marginal must, nevertheless, recognize the existence of a reality to which they are marginal—not only physical space, but historical, social, cultural, and economic realities—that is, the structural dimension of reality. In this way, illiterates have to be recognized as beings "outside of," "marginal to" something, since it is impossible to be marginal to nothing. But being "outside of" or "marginal to" necessarily implies a movement of the one said to be marginal from the center, where he was, to the periphery. This movement, which is an action, presupposes in turn not only an agent but also his reasons. Admitting the existence of men "outside of" or "marginal to" structural reality, we may legitimately ask: who is the author of this movement from the center of the structure to its margin? Do so-called marginal men, among them the illiterates, make the decision to move out to the periphery of society? If so, marginality is an option with all that it involves: hunger, sickness, rickets, pain, mental deficiencies, living death, crime, promiscuity,

despair, the impossibility of being. ... If, then, marginality is not by choice, marginal man has been expelled from and kept outside of the social system and is therefore the object of violence. (*The Politics of Education*, pp. 47–48)

Clearly, though he doesn't follow Fanon into open calls for restorative violence, Freire is speaking in the same radical postcolonial context here, but what he's proposing is also Marxist. Rather blatantly following the ideas of the father of Cultural Marxism, the Hungarian György Lukács,[7] as written in his 1923 book, *History and Class Consciousness*, Freire recognizes the Cultural Marxist axiom that *power lies at the center of society*, from which the entirety can be viewed and moved. (Pause to think of how often you have heard the terms "center" and "decenter" in education-speak in ways that didn't quite seem to make sense before this.)

Freire is saying that colonization, modernization, and industrialization swept in and moved native populations from center to margin, thus unjustly disempowering them, and it did so particularly in their status as *knowers*. Colonial "knowledges" centered themselves and displaced the "knowledges" of the existing people, against their will and as an act of violence. For Freire, the inability to read is intrinsically connected to one's status as marginal in the colonized circumstance. Freire's world is one in which nobody needed to be educated until society changed and began to value formal education, including basic literacy, which unjustly displaced the illiterate (this is the thrust of the first half of the sixth chapter of *The Politics of Education*).

As a highly aggrieved Freire sees it, agrarian peasants, who could neither read nor write, were at the center of their communities until the need to be literate, on someone else's terms, came to dominate

---

7   His name is pronounced, roughly, as English-speakers would pronounce it, "jeurj lou-catch."

society. With this demand, came along with the pressure to get educated so that one can fill a bourgeois-colonizer job on those terms. In other words, a whole new societal apparatus and social machinery for producing and maintaining it came in and displaced what had been before. This is the Marxist-postcolonialist view of colonized and industrial society.

Freire understood that education was implicated in the creation and maintenance of this new world—mostly education on alien terms (say, in Portuguese).[8] Meanwhile, those bourgeois-colonizing people who reordered society using "educated" work as a benchmark, set up a whole new social and professional structure that gets to determine who is and is not sufficiently "educated" to be able to participate in this new upper echelon of society. In turn, they designed "education" itself, including the methods of teaching literacy (especially to adult agrarian peasants), in a way that reproduces and inculcates those values in the students, largely by artificial means (like the Brazilian equivalent of what we, as English speakers, would call "phonics"). This allows them to certify those they wish to admit to "educated" society and to exclude and marginalize those who don't fit the "educated" mold according to their own unjust, if not bogus, standards.

Thus, the standard Marxist conspiracy theory rears its head beneath Freire's project. Freire posits that certain people declared themselves in possession of a special kind of cultural property that privileges them in relation to others, in this case "being educated" or "literate." They used this self-serving claim to structure society so that they are advantaged and others are excluded from that advantage,

---

8   Freire offers a long discussion of this point—too long to quote here—near the end of *The Politics of Education*, discussing the topic of re-Africanizing parts of colonized Africa in a transcribed interview with Donaldo Macedo, his long-time associate and frequent translator into English. The relevant discussion can be found on pp. 182–185 and reveals unambiguous influences of Frantz Fanon (whom he cites directly elsewhere in the book).

estranging the groups from one another and, in fact, from themselves, while plunging them into inextricable societal conflict. He then outlines a way for literacy to be redefined "politically" so that those dispossessed by this imposed structure of society can rebel against it, see themselves as intrinsic knowers in possession of the key knowledge needed to transform society, foster a revolution, and seize the means of defining "literacy" and "education" to enable a more just future in which no one is estranged from self or others. This warped view is the basis for what I am calling Freire's "Marxification of education," which enables the wholesale theft of education by the Critical Pedagogy developed in its wake.

Of note, in his earlier days, before he was exiled from Brazil, Freire understood this arrangement mostly in terms of colonial displacement, although these had Marxist roots and he would have received some Marxist and Liberation Theology ideas from the influence of Dom Hélder Câmara, with whom he first collaborated in 1961 in Recife. (These men met again later in Geneva while Freire was on appointment to the World Council of Churches and Câmara was visiting Switzerland thanks to Klaus Schwab's risky 1974 invitation to the third annual meeting of the European Management Forum, later renamed the World Economic Forum, in Davos.) After his exiles, first from Brazil and then from Bolivia, both in 1964, Freire studied Liberation Theology and Marxism more thoroughly in Chile and adapted these ideas even more deeply into his framework of thought. Both of these systems have to be understood as having provided the underlying framing for Freire's theory of education.

That Freire's entire pedagogy begins from a postcolonialist mindset helps us make sense of an otherwise confusing trend in education today: the *decolonization* phenomenon. The goal of postcolonialism is decolonization. For Freire, the colonization of the knowing system— and thus education and literacy—is at the heart of why education produces and reproduces the stratified and unjust society, including through so-called "humanitarian" educational programs he believes train people to accept that oppression. A decolonized education with a decolonized curriculum relevant to those marginalized by colonialism is therefore necessary to provide them with an authentic education. This assumption of colonized and "decolonizing" curriculum makes its way prominently into education today largely because of Freire (significantly through the work of a later Critical Pedagogue, Joe L. Kincheloe).

A Note on Deeper Philosophical Roots
These radical ideas didn't just spring out of the ground in the 1950s and 1960s fully formed. They have older roots. In the view summarized above, Freire reproduces both Karl Marx and Jean-Jacques Rousseau, from whom these specific Marxist ideas have their roots, and more distantly Giambattista Vico, whom we might consider a key figure in the birth of linguistic-social constructivism and the grand forefather of Freire's emphasis upon "speaking the word to proclaim the world." At any rate, Leftism since Rousseau has been extremely skeptical of the civilized world order—"man is born free, but everywhere he is in chains," being one of Rousseau's most famous remarks—and has fascinated itself with the concept of the noble savage.

Postcolonialism is no exception to this trend and sees the noble pre-colonized "savage" as something that should under all circumstances have been left unsullied by what Europeans had decided constitutes "civilization," which forms the socially constructed "chains" Rousseau complained about. (Marx, incidentally, feels roughly the same about industrialization or, more generally, about the noble worker who is being colonized through the pressures of the division of labor.) These concepts, both in abstract and under colonial realities, are the root of the noble, innocent-as-oppressed character, from the savages of Rousseau through the proletariat of Karl Marx to the minority identities of Woke Marxists. They are the innocents before the Fall of Man, which for Marx arrived with the invention of private property and the division of labor and for the radical postcolonialists came in with the establishment of European civilization as "civilization" itself. For Freire, it's the knower who hasn't had his "concrete" knowledges written over by a colonialist-bourgeois "formal education." (PS: Though it's a topic more appropriate to another volume, this is all modern and postmodern forms of collectivist Gnosticism—the serpent in Genesis 3 warns Eve that she was born free and is nevertheless in "chains" of God's making, maintained by her perpetuated ignorance caused by having been forbidden to acquire knowledge of good and evil, which will set her free. The "bourgeois" arbiters of society in the Marxist reinvention of this mystery religion serve as the intrinsically corrupt and evil demiurge, jailers of Man.)

Though the different philosophies of Rousseau and Marx (and others) deal with these points somewhat differently, they share several deep commonalities central to Leftist thought. They see man as inherently dualistic, with an uncorrupted "true" form trapped inside of the socially conditioned and physically constrained "human being" on the outside (this is "the ghost in the machine"). Yes, even Marx in all his supposed materialism sees the Absolute Man, who is perfectly Socialist and recollects his true nature as a "species-being" that is transcendent of private property, as spiritually dualistic in this way! They all also treat the "noble savage" (or worker, or peasant) as possessing something of an uncorrupted—or, *unfallen*—nobility and, by virtue of the oppression visited upon them, a kind of second sight that would enable people in more civilized, bourgeois, or privileged positions to understand something crucial about the world they inhabit and, in turn, create. All are therefore in the driver's seat of the great dialectical process of History, which is the defining character of Leftism at least since Hegel's death in 1831: savages made to live in cities (Rousseau), Man made (Socialist) to live in Society (Marx), individuals remade to live in society (Critical Marxists), and individual people with group identities made to live as global citizens (Woke Marxists). It was this very idea of Rousseau's, "savages made to live in cities," that was termed *aufheben* in German and thus inspired Hegel, then Marx, and then the rest on down, including Freire and his intellectual inheritors in today's colleges of education and classrooms. For Freire, it is authentic knowers made to live in an ideal democracy, which, for Marxists, only exists under Communism and, for postcolonialists, exists only when every last trace of imperialism and colonialism have been ripped out by the roots.

What's most important to understand from these preceding parts is that Freire's reorganization of education into a Marxist Theory of education, literacy, and even knowing exists within a long current of "Dialectical Leftist" thought extending back to the middle of the 18th century and comprising many branches that occasionally separate and recombine. These points are made mostly for historical and philosophical context, however, and are not the thrust of what Freire did to education or what his schools are doing to our kids.

Freire's Key Books

Paulo Freire published, or had published in his name, about a million books,[9] though probably four of them are the most significant. Freire's most famous book, by far, is his second major piece, his 1968 work, *Pedagogy of the Oppressed* (its first publication, however, was in English in 1970). This book is given pride of place in virtually every, if not literally every, education program in North America today. In it, he lays out the basic tenets of his philosophy of education, which is essentially Marxist, postcolonial, and based upon a few simple concepts, which we will detail thoroughly in subsequent sections.

In it, particularly, he challenges the prevailing notion of education (which one might guess is the Prussian model), characterizing it as

---

9   Truly, dozens.

a "banking model" of education. This, he claims, treats students as though they are bank deposit boxes into which teachers place knowledge upon which the students can later capitalize, or not. His program is unabashedly radical, as he summarizes neatly in *Pedagogy of the Oppressed* in an oft-quoted passage in modern education books:

> [T]he more radical the person is, the more fully he or she enters into reality so that, knowing it better, he or she can better transform it. This individual is not afraid to confront, to listen, to see the world unveiled. This person is not afraid to meet the people or to enter into dialogue with them. This person does not consider himself or herself the proprietor of history or of all people, or the liberator of the oppressed; but he or she does commit himself or herself, within history, to fight at their side. (p. 39)

This statement, like many in Freire's work, is meant to orient toward the Left those who take up his work or any of the many education books now based in his radical pedagogy. In my opinion, however, despite its reach, status, and citation count, *Pedagogy of the Oppressed* is by no means Freire's most influential work nor his clearest exposition of his theory of education. That designation goes to his 1985 book, *The Politics of Education: Culture, Power, and Liberation*, because it resulted in his work, including the earlier *Pedagogy of the Oppressed*, being brought into American colleges of education. Though *Pedagogy of the Oppressed* and Freire's works more broadly were known to the American audience before 1985—indeed, he lectured at Harvard in the late 1960s— they were only taken seriously throughout colleges in education after a favorable but short review of *The Politics of Education* in the *Harvard Education Review* in the year of its publication. In that regard, *The Politics of Education* subsumes in total impact most of the earlier (and vaguer)

Pedagogy of the Oppressed.[10] (And, at any rate, the books do not say much different—if nothing else, Marxist Theory is profoundly simple once you get under the hood, and its exposition mostly involves endlessly repeating the same thing in slightly different phrasing that its authors seem to find clever.)

Paulo Freire Comes to America

Freire, the man, was first brought to the United States in 1967 by two priests, Monsignor Robert J. Fox and Father Joseph Fitzpatrick (who was later embroiled in a child sex-abuse scandal), through the connection of the radical progressive priest Ivan Illich, champion of the "deschooling" movement. The purpose was to oversee the minority-community schools Fox was experimenting with in New York City. Shortly after this introduction onto the American scene, Harvard University offered Freire a two-year lecturer position. He accepted, sort of. Freire took the lecture position at Harvard for only six months in 1969 so he could also accept an appointment to the ecumenical interfaith organization, the World Council of Churches in Geneva. It was during the beginning of his long exile from Brazil—first to Bolivia in 1964, then to Chile soon after—that Freire, then a radical postcolonialist and experimental adult-literacy educator, was thoroughly brought into Marxist thought, mostly through contacts with various Liberation Theologians (that is, Marxists posing as Catholics). He also wrote his first major book, *Education as the Practice of Freedom* (1967), and *Pedagogy of the Oppressed* (1968) in exile.

This network of priests was also instrumental in bringing Freire and his work to the United States, particularly Harvard. Once there, Freire's work had a modest impact that wasn't far-reaching. He had

---

10 To mention them, the four Freirean books that stand out in importance are *Education as the Practice of Freedom* (1967), *Pedagogy of the Oppressed* (1970), *The Politics of Education* (1985), and *Pedagogy of Hope* (1992), which is strongly autobiographical.

his short appointment to lecture at Harvard, invitations to write a few articles for the *Harvard Educational Review* that received only a little attention, and a few mentions in Critical Education Theorists' books as they brought Marxist critique to bear on educational theory and practice. His reception remained tepid and his ideas marginal until Henry Giroux encountered his work in the mid-1970s.

Giroux was, at the time, a very frustrated Critical and Leftist high school teacher in the upper-middle-class suburb of Barrington, Rhode Island. He was struggling to have his radical (read: crackpot) methodology and classroom approaches accepted by his school and, later, colleges of education, notably Boston University, which denied him tenure very probably for being a radical—in fact, an open Communist. In the midst of this struggle in the latter half of the 1970s, Giroux was given a copy of *Pedagogy of the Oppressed* and had what can only be described as a Road-to-Damascus–level conversion event into the Freirean religion of Marxism centered upon education. Here's how he describes it in a personal reflection in written in 2008:

> I was a high school teacher and I found myself in a class trying to do all kinds of innovative things and the vice principal came up and he said I don't want the students sitting in a circle, I want them, you know, in a straight line and blah blah blah, and I didn't have an answer for that. I didn't have the theoretical language, and ironically, a week earlier somebody had given me a copy of *Pedagogy of the Oppressed*, and I was so frustrated that I went home, read the book. I stayed up all night, got dressed in the morning, went to school. I felt my life had literally changed. And it's fair to say that certainly Paulo Freire, for me, to talk about the origins of this movement in the United States, while you can talk about Dewey and the social reconstructionists, who talked about critical democracy and education but really did never really talk about critical pedagogy, Paulo's work is really the first to mark that moment. The [Critical

Pedagogy] archive really should begin there. (quoted in *The Critical Turn in Education*, pp. 74–75)

Immediately, Giroux struck up a correspondence with Freire, forged a relationship, and began to work tirelessly at his "praxis" of getting Freirean ideas and "democratic education" firmly lodged, if not centered, in North American colleges of education and other education circles. Giroux connected with Freire in person in 1983, and their relationship led to frequent American visits by Freire. With the publication of *The Politics of Education* in 1985, through Giroux's relentless evangelism (including his gushing introduction in that book) and diligent "praxis" of getting Marxists radicals tenured in colleges of education, by the end of the 1980s, Freire was a central fixture of North American ed schools. By 1992, Gottesman observes, "Freire had emerged, where he stands today, everywhere" (*The Critical Turn in Education*, p. 25). As he elaborates,

As even a cursory glance at literature in the field makes clear, over the past 25 years *Pedagogy of the Oppressed* has become the citation for signaling a scholar's belief in education as an emancipatory process within an unjust social order. And, significantly, it is the word 'critical' that tends to trigger the citation. (p. 26)

This is the key to understanding Freire, then. What Freire brought to education is that you have to learn to see structural oppression as a Critical Marxist if you have any hope of building a movement to overthrow it. Even radicals, progressives, and classical Marxists in education in the North American context didn't have this piece, and neither did the radical neo-Marxists in the 1960s. This "educational" process in which education and politics are dialectically synthesized into one activity is *instrumental* to Marxism in the free, liberal West because, frankly, that structural oppression isn't actually there, at least not significantly. You have to be groomed into seeing it through an "educational" process, and that's what Freire offers. Freire, then, is in a meaningful sense the father of Woke because going Woke means *learning to see structural oppression* in virtually everything *in order to denounce it*, like a process of waking up to a hidden, horrible world. Freireans assume the oppression is there and then aim to groom "learners" to see it.

On The Politics of Education

The Politics of Education is a curious book, to be sure. The book is essentially an edited collection of essays by Freire, apparently written originally between 1970 and 1985, and five of the first six chapters in the book explain the basic ideas of his pedagogy (theory of education) in greater clarity, detail, and brevity than does *Pedagogy of the Oppressed*. The exception is the fifth chapter, which discusses the role of the social worker, characterizing social workers and teachers both as types of educators whose duty it is to generate political literacy in those they assist. In my opinion, this chapter foreshadows the widespread implementation of Social-Emotional Learning (SEL), particularly "Tranformative SEL" (which matches Freire's terminology, tone, and intention quite closely), by opening the door to think of teachers as *de facto* social workers who are to intervene in the social and emotional lives and processes of their students in addition to aiding their academic development. Education activist Linda Darling-Hammond, something of the mother of SEL implementation in the United States, quotes Freire plainly on this point in her foreword to the 2015 *Handbook of Social and Emotional Learning: Research and Practice* (p. xii). For Freire, however, the point of all such instruction is unambiguously *political* generally and *to generate a Marxist consciousness* specifically. Entire chapters in his 1985 book are dedicated explicitly to these themes being, for Freire, the true-but-hidden point of education.

The subsequent five chapters in this book get positively wild for a book on pedagogy. Chapter 7 is devoted to the idea of the crucial role and process of (Marxist) conscientization (i.e., thought reform), expresses the need for Leftist utopianism, and literally upholds the guerrilla murderer Che Guevara as an ideal figure representing these concepts (and *love*—a huge theme for Freire) when put into practice. Chapter 8 is devoted to replacing practical or functional education with political education, calls explicitly for perpetual cultural revolution as the goal of true education, and advocates that educators and learners have to die and be reborn in their own Marxist "Easter" to do their jobs correctly. Chapter 10 elaborates on this blatantly theological idea considerably, drops much of the pretense, and is wholly devoted to Liberation Theology and the connection to the Church, which is seen as another educational domain hardly different from schools. Chapter 9, in between, forwards a profoundly Marxist notion of the deeper purpose of education under a banner of "humanistic education," which should be understood in the sense Marx meant when he explained that his approach is meant to humanize the world, society, and man. Chapter 11 is a short word of praise for the unique character (read: charlatan) of James Cone, famous for his Black Liberation Theology, which is some kind of hybrid of Liberation Theology, the Social Gospel of the Fabian Baptist Walter Rauschenbusch, and Black Liberationism (a postcolonialist and neo-Marxist precursor to Critical Race Theory).

Paulo Freire, Liberation Theologian

The religious tone in this book is so explicit and central to Freire's pedagogy that Henry Giroux, in his introduction to the book, remarks that Freire's is a "permanent prophetic vision" for what education means and might achieve. This language echoes Freire's call that churches, like schools, must become wholly remade in his image, at which point they become "the prophetic church" (which prophesies a liberated Utopia). In fact, it bears reading how Giroux describes Freire's work in the introduction he wrote for *The Politics of Education*:

> As the reader will discover in this book, Freire is a harsh critic of the reactionary church. At the same time, he situates his faith and sense of hope in the God of history and of the oppressed, whose teachings make it impossible, in Freire's words, to "reconcile Christian love with the exploitation of human beings."
>
> Within the discourse of theologies of liberation, Freire fashions a powerful theoretical antidote to the cynicism and despair of many left radical critics. The utopian character of his analysis is concrete in its nature and appeal, and takes as its starting point collective actors in their various historical settings and the particularity of their problems and forms of oppression. It is utopian only in the sense that it refuses to surrender to the risks and dangers that face all challenges to dominant power structures. It is prophetic in that it views the kingdom of God as something to be created on earth but only through a faith in both other human beings and the necessity of permanent struggle. The notion of faith that emerges in Freire's work is informed by the memory of the oppressed, the suffering that must not be allowed to continue, and the need to never forget that the prophetic vision is an ongoing process, a vital aspect of the very nature of human life. In short, by combining the discourses of critique and possibility Freire joins history and theology in order to provide the theoretical basis for a radical pedagogy that combines hope, critical reflection, and collective struggle. (*The Politics of Education*, pp. xvii–xviii)

Oddly for a paradigm-shifting education book, this book is frequently this explicitly religious in character. As noted, for example, in chapters 8 and 10, Freire explicitly claims that to be effective, teachers must personally live through a kind of existential "Easter" that awakens them to a full Marxist political consciousness (otherwise, they are "necrophiliac," death-loving, as used by the neo-Marxist psychologist Erich Fromm, whom Freire cites). In fact, he says this is the only true meaning of Easter and that without it Christians (as well as educators) merely go through dead rhetoric that turns the event into just another date on the calendar. Freire, then, is literally calling the existing society and Christian church a death cult and any functional educational system within it a mode of maintaining and reproducing that evil. His answer is equally religious: calling to remake education and the churches entirely as an opposing form of religious education into political consciousness "on the side of the oppressed." To accomplish this, he specifically calls upon educators to die to the existing order of society and resurrect themselves as people with (Marxist) consciousness. They can then share this with their students. This is sufficiently bizarre in an educational theory book, especially one of this degree of influence in an explicitly legally secular society, to merit quoting directly at some length from the tenth chapter:

> This new apprenticeship will violently break down the elitist concept of existence they had absorbed while being ideologized. The *sine qua non* the apprenticeship demands is that, first of all, they really experience their own Easter, that they die as elitists so as to be resurrected on the side of the oppressed, that they be born again with the beings who were not allowed to be. Such a process implies a renunciation of myths that are dear to them: the myth of their superiority, of their purity of soul, of their virtues, their wisdom, the myth that they save the poor, the myth of the neutrality of the church, of theology, education, science, technology, the myth of their own impartiality. From these grow the other myths: of the inferiority of other people, of their spiritual and physical impurity, and of the absolute ignorance of the oppressed.

This Easter, which results in the changing of consciousness, must be existentially experienced. The real Easter is not commemorative rhetoric. It is praxis; it is historical involvement. The old Easter of rhetoric is dead—with no hope of resurrection. It is only in the authenticity of historical praxis that Easter becomes the death that makes life possible. But the bourgeois world view, basically necrophiliac (death-loving) and therefore static, is unable to accept this supremely biophiliac (life-loving) experience of Easter. The bourgeois mentality—which is far more than just a convenient abstraction—kills the profound historical dynamism of Easter and turns it into no more than a date on the calendar.

The lust to possess, a sign of the necrophiliac world view, rejects the deeper meaning of resurrection. Why should I be interested in rebirth if I hold in my hands, as objects to be possessed, the torn body and soul of the oppressed? I can only experience rebirth at the side of the oppressed by being born again, with them, in the process of liberation. I cannot turn such a rebirth into a means of *owning* the world, since it is essentially a means of *transforming* the world. (*The Politics of Education*, pp. 122–123)

For those who know what they are looking at, this is a replacement of the Christian theological beliefs regarding the central event of their faith, the death and resurrection of Jesus Christ, with a blatantly Marxist counterfeit in which the individual dies to the existing world and is resurrected into a Marxist (conscious "Socialist Man")—his own Marxist "Christ." For Freire, this creates a new Commission for the churches, which he sees as operating as parallel educational institutions, hence their inclusion in this book on educational theory and practice. He writes,

[N]o church can be really prophetic if it remains the haven of the masses or the agent of modernization and conservation. The prophetic church is no home for the oppressed, alienating them further by empty denunciations. On the contrary. it invites them to a new Exodus. Nor is the prophetic church one that chooses modernization and thereby does no more than stagnate. Christ was no conservative. The prophetic church, like him, must move forward constantly, forever dying and forever being reborn. In order to be, it must always be in a state of *becoming*. The prophetic church must also accept an existence that is in dramatic tension between past and future, staying and going, speaking the word and keeping silence, being and not being. There is no prophecy without risk. (*The Politics of Education*, p. 139)

This heresy is not just a blurring of the boundaries between school and churches, it's also an advancement of Liberation Theology and a repurposing of that Marxist faith into educational theory and practice. The Liberation Theologians in South America, including the infamous Marxist "Red Bishop" of Freire's own Recife, Brazil, Dom Hélder Câmara (whom Freire defends by name in a footnote in *The Politics of Education*), are clearly among his chief influences. Incidentally, as it happens, Câmara had at least two other remarkably famous proteges who were profoundly influenced by his take on Liberation Theology: the Argentinian who would later become Pope Francis and Executive Chairman of the World Economic Forum and political protege of Henry Kissinger, Professor Klaus Schwab.

It is at this point that I must remind you that Freire's intention with this unsettling Easter passage is to insist that this Marxist "Easter" is a necessary precondition for any who want to be religious leaders or educators. He then says it is the educator's role to bring this cult-religious transformation through rebirth to their student "learners." This is the unambiguous replacement of education with what the Chinese Communists termed "brainwashing." Thus, it is at *this* point that I must also remind you that this is written in the book that changed the course of North American colleges of education and our legally secular public education system to make them into what they are today. It is on the back of this instruction that our education system has been remade (in the "real Easter" of "historical praxis" that "the bourgeois mentality" cannot accept) such that *almost all of our kids go to Paulo Freire's schools.*

Becoming as Marxist Gods

The blatantly religious tone is consistent throughout Freire's work. For example, we have already mentioned Freire's insistence that education should be about "learning to speak the word to proclaim the world," which is the unique role of God in the Bible. Freire is quite explicit about this role being the role of the man who wishes to transform society according to Marxist Theory, though. Take the way he opens chapter 3 of *Pedagogy of the Oppressed*, where he touches upon this subject specifically:

> As we attempt to analyze dialogue as a human phenomenon, we discover something which is the essence of dialogue itself: *the word.* But the word is more than just an instrument which makes dialogue possible; accordingly, we must seek its constitutive elements. Within the word we find two dimensions, reflection and action, in such radical interaction that if one is sacrificed—even in part—the other immediately suffers. There is no true word that is not at the same time a praxis. Thus, to speak a true word is to transform the world.
>
> An unauthentic word, one which is unable to transform reality, results when dichotomy is imposed upon its constitutive elements. When a word is deprived of its dimension of action, reflection automatically suffers as well; and the word is changed into idle chatter, into *verbalism,* into an alienated and alienating "blah." It becomes an empty word, one which cannot denounce the world,

for denunciation is impossible without a commitment to transform, and there is no transformation without action. (p. 87)

What you've just read is literally a logocentric rendering of the Marxist Theology—marking a dialectical return toward Vico's praxis through declarative language and Hegel's idealism. Education, for Freire, is going to be a process of learning to "transform reality," which is the essential Marxist project.

> As an event calling forth the critical reflection of both the learners and educators, the literacy process must relate *speaking the word* to *transforming reality*, and to man's role in this transformation. Perceiving the significance of that relationship is indispensable for those learning to read and write if we are really committed to liberation. (*The Politics of Education*, p. 51)

Indeed, according to both Freire and Marx, transforming reality is what makes men human and not mere animals—a key existential (and theological) point.

> If, for animals, orientation in the world means adaptation to the world, for man it means humanizing the world by transforming it. For animals there is no historical sense, no options or values in their orientation in the world; for man there is both an historical and a value dimension. Men have the sense of "project," in contrast to the instinctive routines of animals. (*The Politics of Education*, p. 44)

Christian sensibilities aside, one is forced by his own words to conclude that Freire is much more a religious figure than an education theorist, and his educational program is far nearer to explicit religious instruction than it is to educational theory at all. Thus, to the degree that this pedagogy has informed public schools in the United States and its fifty states, one might suspect it butts up against a heretofore unrecognized Establishment Clause challenge. Visible are a conception of the world, life in it, and its ultimate questions such that duties of conscience arise from the belief system. These points, though, are the usual criteria for recognizing a belief system as a religion according to First Amendment jurisprudence on the U.S. Constitution. These, the state cannot mandate or compel. That's a matter for a deeper debate in another forum, however.

Before turning completely away from that debate, however, let's note that it is explicit in Freire's project in a way that's perplexing many contemporary thinkers. Freire opens the sixth chapter of *The Politics of Education* with a short, curiously philosophical section titled "Every Educational Practice Implies a Concept of Man and the World" (p. 43). This is a bit of philosophical sleight of hand (sleight of mind?) upon which all the rest of his work is justified. The essential claim in it is that there's no such thing as a neutral approach to education because they all rest upon (political) value judgments rooted in an underlying concept of man and the world. He then declares the Marxist theology the only valid concept of man and the world, just without saying so explicitly:

> Experience teaches us not to assume that the obvious is clearly understood. So it is with the truism with which we begin: All educational practice implies a theoretical stance on the educator's part. This stance in turn implies—sometimes more, sometimes less explicitly—an interpretation of man and the world. It could not be otherwise. The process of men's orientation in the world involves not just the association of sense images, as for animals. It involves, above all, thought-language, that is, the possibility of the act of knowing through his praxis, by which man transforms reality. For man, this process of orientation in the world can be understood neither as a purely subjective event, nor as an objective or mechanistic

one, but only as an event in which subjectivity and objectivity are united. Orientation in the world, so understood, places the question of the purposes of action at the level of critical perception of reality. (*The Politics of Education*, pp. 43–44)

This isn't, then, a mere question of whether education is "values-neutral," as Critical Pedagogues often assert it cannot be (and their critics are often forced to accept, putting them on Marxist turf). This is a question of the insertion of an entire *worldview*, not mere values, on what amounts to a complete intellectual swindle (standard for Marxism).

That swindle is unmasked by realizing that Freire is effectively saying the Marxist dialectical framing "in which subjectivity and objectivity are united" is the true framing for reality, and people are either more or less explicitly aware of this "fact," which Freire asserts is "self-evident." Of course, as we already see, this worldview is the Marxist theology. The intellectual swindle is accomplished by insisting that everyone else is just unaware of how reality really works, which is why they cannot see that it's "self-evident," and therefore are unqualified to guide any educational process as compared to a Freirean educator. The "self-evident" nature of this framing is only visible, however, once one accepts it and is precisely the same intellectual swindle effected by Karl Marx in *The Economic and Philosophic Manuscripts* (1844) for forcing acceptance of his identical concept of man and the world. Thus, Freire reproduces the lie that lurks beneath all Marxist thought.

In practical terms, this means that debating whether or not education can or should be "values-neutral" misses the point, typically to the advantage of the Marxist (or other relativist). The question isn't about values. The question is about an underlying theory of man and the world. Values exist *within* those broad conceptions that bind and orient other philosophies (like a theory of values, called an axiology), which are called "theologies" when they are pointed toward a conception of the Divine.

In the West, we have accepted a *liberal*—not *Leftist*—theory of man and the world, which, most importantly, contains within it liberty of conscience (enshrined in the American First Amendment). Leftism, notably, does *not* afford that liberty and therefore must not be confused with liberalism, which is the philosophical school the United States was founded upon.

Under that basic, humility-oriented frame, the state *cannot* determine for individuals what conception of man and the world to advance beyond a very rudimentary basic framework that actually *is* self-evident—we're beings capable of reason in some limited fashion who, as a result, have certain inalienable rights that are secured so that we cannot have forced upon us some more specific conception of man and the world. Our capacity for reason makes us human, and therefore the state cannot dictate to us *what our capacity for reason is purposed for*, if anything, whether that be to serve and glorify God, submit to Allah, transcend worldly suffering through the Eightfold Path and reach Nirvana, or ascertain the subject-object dialectic so that we realize ourselves to be transformative subjects working to build the world into a Marxist Utopia.

This isn't a question of *values* at all, then. It's a question of how values are determined in the first place. State endorsement of Freirean education, which assumes the Marxist dialectical concept explicitly, which says our being is such that we are meant to transform the world for particular ends (including building the kingdom of God here on Earth), is therefore an *unambiguous* First Amendment violation in the United States in the same way that endorsing an explicitly Christian concept of man and the world would be. In fact, under a Freirean concept, it would not be possible for a Christian to believe in God in any way other than as given in (Woke) Liberation Theology, which unambiguously violates their rights—a point Freire makes rather clear regarding "the prophetic church" throughout chapter ten of *The Politics of Education*! (Note well, *private* Freirean schools can exist just fine in the United States, then, just as other private religious schools can, subject to the same laws and policies as any other religious school, *and* they should be recognized—and declared—as such.)

—

Now, having gained some idea of who Paulo Freire is and what his work entails, we turn our attention to the major concepts of his pedagogy. The essentials can be captured in five of Freire's key concepts: what I refer to as the "Marxification" of education, "conscientization," the "generative themes" approach, "codification and decodification," and the "dialogical method." Those familiar with education as it is taught and practiced throughout North America will find at least the last three of these immediately recognizable, if not familiar, though in slightly modernized forms. The first two are essentially a repurposing of Marxism and neo-Marxism, including the Maoist program of thought reform, into the educational arena.

In the following chapters, the reader is asked to endure a particular literary annoyance with a modicum of patience, as I'm forced to repeat several quotations from Freire, sometimes a few times between now and the end of the book. This regretful decision was made not to be repetitive or boring or for lack of illustrative source material but to draw different points out of the key paragraphs of Freire's works differently as they fit in the differing contexts of the forthcoming chapters I've split and organized his program into for the purposes of this presentation. My hope is, then, that it adds clarity and that the modest annoyance proves to be worth it.

III.

THE MARXIFICATION OF EDUCATION

Paulo Freire Marxified education itself. That is, he turned pedagogy into a Marxist Theory and turned the very concepts of education, literacy, and knowledge into sites of Marxian social analysis. This is not equivalent to inserting Marxism or Marxist ideas into curricula, nor is it the same as revamping education into a Marxist indoctrination, as many believe. It is a far deeper shift in the theory of education that has redefined how we educate our students throughout the United States and now around the world. As noted, the closest parallel is to the brainwashing thought reform in Maoist re-education prisons and schools. The theft of education we have been discussing is enabled by precisely this Marxification, which repurposes education *from within*.

An Introduction to Marxism as a Mode of Thought

For those not familiar, a general overview of Marxist Theory (read: theology) is in order. In simplest possible terms, Marxism can be presented in two pieces. The first of these is a general theory of how class society operates, and the second of these is what can be done about it. The first is Marx's peculiar dialectical conception of the world, view of the Absolute Man, and conflict-oriented sociology, and the second is the seizing of the means of production to transform society according to its (Marxist) ultimate purpose.

Marx's view of how class society is organized and operates, in greatest generality, posits the existence of a special kind of "bourgeois" property to which some people grant themselves access while excluding everyone else. This access "stratifies" society into a class that has and a class that does not have access to the special property. These classes are intrinsically in conflict with one another, as the upper class erects a system that estranges the everyday individual (for Marx, the worker) from the product of his efforts and thus his ability to fully and truly be. Those with the power to do so (currently referred to as "privilege") generate elaborate mythologies, called "ideology," that justify their power. Marx claimed that ideology "mystifies" reality and that Marxism "demystifies" it.

This special property and structural class stratification around it create a number of consequences. First, because those with access hope to maintain it and to keep it exclusive, society is separated into oppressors, who have the privilege of access to the special property, and the oppressed, who are excluded from it. Those with access constitute a "superstructural" layer of society, which means they have access to shape the future course of history. Those excluded access constitute the human capital base of society (man reduced to animal or machine through the division of labor), which defines its functional "infrastructure" that makes it work and produces most or all of the legitimate value that drives society. These are in "dialectical" relationship—fitting into the human component of a vast mythology of reality called "dialectical materialism" that allegedly explains the evolution of everything in the universe, including man and society. The superstructure rests upon the base and defines itself in relation to exploiting it in order to maintain its privileged status. This relationship is therefore inherently antagonistic and dynamic and generates a pervasive "structure" of society that orders its affairs and defines its social relations—something like a materialist "spirit" (*Geist*) that pervades and shapes reality and experience.

Those social relations in society (which are socially constructed, obviously) in turn delimit the range of subjective comprehension people within that society have. Those who are oppressed within the dynamic are conditioned to accept their oppression because the range of their imagination is limited to the world they're forced to occupy. This steals what makes them essentially human from them and forces them to live in an "alien," thus alienating, world. Lacking comprehension of that world prevents them from being able to change it, especially since they are not in the superstructural layer of society from which society's direction is determined. Those in the privileged class are either naively or willfully blind to the arrangement they benefit from and are therefore also limited in their subjective range in a way that only the oppressed could possibly cure them of (oppression confers *gnosis* of Man's true Social nature). Marxist consciousness, derived from what Marx called "Scientific Socialism" (*Wissenschaftlicher Sozialismus*), is not only the only antidote to this limitation on subjective consciousness; it's also billed as the only true "scientific" study of man, society, and history itself.

Man's role in this is to realize his true nature, to understand the "concrete" conditions of his structured life, and to change these conditions toward the Socialist. This society-changing activity is called "praxis," which derives from the Greek root for the word "practice." Praxis means a creative act for which the means and ends are not distinct, as opposed to poeisis (that is, poetic) activity, in which they are distinct—think of the difference between building a house (poeisis) and a home (praxis), or schooling (poesis) and educating (praxis). For Marx, Man builds Society through his theory-informed praxis (that is, committed activism), and in turn, through social conditioning, Society shapes and delimits Man in what is known as "the inversion of praxis." Marxism can be thought of as a philosophy of learning to see the world in terms of this allegedly self-perpetuating, stable social cycle and then destabilizing it and seizing the means of its production in order to redirect it toward the desired end, Communism, which Marx believed captures Man's true nature as a fully social "species-being," from which he has been estranged by the division of society caused by the establishment of a special form of property and a myth of privileged access to it (for him, the division of labor and private property).

So, the privileged class maintains this structural "reality" by creating a broad social mythology justifying their access, called an "ideology." (Marxism bills itself as the sole path to "the end of ideology"—not this ideology or that ideology, but *ideology* itself, *in toto*.) These circumstances, reinforced by the persuasive power of the ideology, *structure* society in such a way that these circumstances maintain themselves, particularly so that the privileged remain privileged and the oppressed remain oppressed—that is, they become the fundamental organizing principle of an unjust society. Ideology functions in such a way as to ensure neither group is conscious of the true nature of society. The goal, however, as Marx and Engels note in *The Communist Manifesto* can be summarized in the single idea of "abolition of private property" of this special kind.

This basic structure of Marxism repeats itself through every evolution of Marxist Theory.

- For Marx, the special property was *capital*. Its ideology was *capitalism*, a caricature of market economies. Its winners are the *bourgeoisie* and its losers the *working class*, who become a *proletariat* when awakened to *class consciousness*. The structure of this society is enforced by structural *classism* which is *materially deterministic*. The goal of Marx's economic-material Marxism is the *abolition (or transcendence) of private property*.
- In Critical Race Theory, as I argue in *Race Marxism*, the special property is *whiteness*. Its ideology is *white supremacy*. Its winners are *whites* and *white-adjacents*. Its losers are *people of color*. Either of these can become *antiracists* when awakened to *race consciousness* (instead of colorblindness). The structure of this society is

enforced by *systemic racism,* which is both *materially* and *structurally deterministic.* Its goal is the *abolition (or transcendence) of whiteness.*

- In Queer Theory, the special property is *normalcy.* Its ideology is *cisheteronormativity,* that it is regarded as normal to be straight and not trans. Its winners are *cisheterosexuals* and *people who pass as such.* Its losers are *the abnormal.* These can become *allies* or *queer* when awakened with *queer consciousness.* The structure of this society is enforced by *homophobia, transphobia,* and other *bigotries of normativity,* which are both *materially* and *structurally deterministic.* Its goal is *the abolition (or transcendence) of normalcy and, with it, normativity,* i.e., all norms and socially enforced categorical expectations.

- For Freire, the special property is *formal education* or *literacy.* Its ideology is one of "educated society," which values being *educated* and *literate* in ways acceptable to the existing system. Its winners are the *formally educated* and *literate,* regarded as *knowers,* and its losers the *illiterate,* who are actually knowers in their own right, though the system excludes them, their ways of knowing, and their knowledges. They are awakened through *political literacy,* and *conscientization* is the process of their awakening. The *critically conscious* or *conscientized* are those who have been awakened. The structure of this society is enforced by expectations on *literacy* and *formal education,* which are *materially* and *structurally deterministic,* relegating the underclass to a "culture of silence," as Freire has it. The goal is *the abolition (or transcendence) of formal education and objective knowledge,* and thus the immediate goal is the reappropriation of education into a process of conscientiation and "humanization."

Being conscientized (in any Marxist construct) is not merely being made aware of the conditions and organization of class society as Marxists see them. It goes deeper. It also includes realizing that as conscious subjects, even those in the underclass are makers of History. More than that, they play a special and certain role in ensuring History evolves toward its intended (Socialist) end. Thus, not only are the oppressed makers of History, they're *privileged* makers of History who have been estranged from that essential fact about themselves and are therefore unjustly disempowered.

Secondly, then, Marx proposes that conscientization *must* lead to action, specifically with regard to the means of production—that is, praxis. For Marx, Man is a product of the society in which he finds himself, but Man, in turn, creates the society in which he lives, ideally through his conscious praxis. Thus, man can bumble along unconscious and keep repeating the same ideological beliefs, which reproduces the existing society, or he can awaken and seize the means of production of society, thus man.[11] That is, man makes himself by making the (material, for Marx; knowledge for Freire) conditions of his society and can allow this to keep happening blindly, to the advantage of the privileged, or consciously.

In some sense, the Marxist sees three possible evolutionary courses for society. In a truly primitive or otherwise naive state, it might evolve organically, following something like a "natural selection" process where the pressures of social life (within and between political entities like nations) lead to decisions being made that shape its course. On the other hand, since we don't live in a truly naive or primitive state— Rousseau's imposition of society bears on this thinking—we are actually in a kind of "artificial selection" state of societal evolution where those who have granted themselves access to society's superstructure direct its course for their own benefit in varying degrees of consciousness to this fact. Thirdly, the evolution of society can be seized by the conscious and turned into an intentional artificial selection toward a better set of conditions that improves Society, Man, and the world in

---

11 Yes, seeking to control this intentionally and to a purpose is a form of eugenics.

which he finds himself—that is, consciously *transforming* it toward a desired (Socialist) end. Typically, Marxist-type thinkers discount the possibility of the first of these three and argue that we therefore have a choice, with no neutrality available to us, to side with them or to allow oppression (fascism) to continue because the fundamental fact of the purposed shaping of Society and Man is happening regardless.

Of course, consciously directing the evolution of Society and Man toward a desired end is a form of eugenics, and the Marxists seem to understand this in their usual backwards way. That can be glimpsed in the fact that they call everything else a form of eugenics because they think we live in an artificially selected social environment that benefits the few at the expense of the many—it's always already happening through the "bad" people unless the means of production are seized by the "good" people. (Also of course, this reveals Marxist thought to be a gigantic conspiracy theory.) Because they believe they alone chart the path to ending all such ideological drives, they think their eugenics program doesn't count and is therefore the only true anti-eugenics program possible since we simply cannot return to a primitive state of Nature.

How this plays out in Freirean education, for what it's worth, is replacing conditions with knowledge, transmitted through education. We could, perhaps, learn organically, except we have Society. Therefore, we learn falsely and in the best interests of those who have set themselves up in power through their claims to knowledge. Alternatively, we could accept alternative knowledges and ways of knowing selected for their political utility in moving Society toward its intended end, which is a liberated (Socialist) Utopia. Any other choice produces all this evil since the knowledge genie is already out of the bottle.

In Marxist Theory, those with privilege won't let it go easily, though, so this transition from "oppressive" and "domesticating" artificial selection to "liberating" and "utopian" (Marxist) artificial selection must proceed via revolution and an enforced, administered State ruled by the now-conscious underclass—a *dictatorship of the proletariat*. In Critical Race Theory, a functional dictatorship of the anti-racists, as described by Ibram X. Kendi, for example, in *Politico Magazine* fulfills this goal.[12] In Queer Theory, relentless deconstruction of all categories and norms through queer activism does. In Freirean education, all education becomes a *political education*, with educators as facilitators into (critical, or Marxist) consciousness, so that all knowledge becomes political knowledge understood on Marxist terms. In fact, Freire goes on in *The Politics of Education* to explain that true education is political education (specifically, true "literacy" is political literacy) "facilitated" by conscientized teachers. This is what the Marxists have achieved in our schools over the last forty years.

Political Literacy and the Knowing Field

Teaching Marxism or Marxist ideas or even indoctrinating students in Marxism is something that might occur within some other pedagogical framework suited to teaching children. This is not what Paulo Freire offers. For Freire, the very concept of being "educated" or "literate" (I will use these interchangeably), or being a "knower," is something that must be understood in a Marxist way, roughly as outlined above.

In short, Freire builds a pedagogical architecture in which those in powerful, privileged, bourgeois, or otherwise advantaged positions in society decide what it means to be "educated," "literate," and "knowing" in such a way that it structures society to their own advantage while oppressing the underclass of "uneducated," "illiterate" people, who are not *regarded as* "knowers," outside that structure. Those outside of the structure are, by virtue of their (political) illiteracy, kept in

---

12 https://www.politico.com/interactives/2019/how-to-fix-politics-in
-america/inequality/pass-an-anti-racist-constitutional-amendment/

a "culture of silence," in which they cannot speak (politically) or will not be heard if they try. This state prevents them from *being*, according to Freire, an extreme claim only comprehensible in the language of Marxism. Being a Man, in Marxism, means knowing you have the capacity to transform reality according to your subjective vision and state of conscientization.

> In the culture of silence the masses are mute, that is, they are prohibited from creatively taking part in the transformations of their society and therefore prohibited from being. Even if they can occasionally read and write because they were "taught" in humanitarian—but not humanist—literacy campaigns, they are nevertheless alienated from the power responsible for their silence. (*The Politics of Education*, p. 50)

In keeping with the central theological conceit of Marxism, Freire calls his remedy to this characterization of what is now sometimes called "the knowing field" a "humanizing" education. He distinguishes that from "humanitarian" education programs that seem to care about the illiterate and aim to teach them to read *words* but not their political context. Such campaigns claim to teach the underprivileged necessary educational skills, but in fact also condition them to accept the unjust terms of their societies. Those humanitarian literacy campaigns perpetuate the culture of silence, according to Freire, because they do not teach what actually needs to be taught to achieve true literacy, which is political literacy.

> Critically speaking, illiteracy is neither an "ulcer" nor a "poison herb" to be eradicated, nor a "disease." Illiteracy is one of the concrete expressions of an unjust social reality. Illiteracy is not a strictly linguistic or exclusively pedagogical or methodological problem. It is political, as is the very literacy through which we try to overcome

illiteracy. Dwelling naively or astutely on intelligence does not affect
in the least the intrinsic politics. (*The Politics of Education*, p. 10)

Here, we see, for Freire, the construction of the Marxification of education and literacy, which is to be understood not as a state of capacity but as a political circumstance. Freire indicates he means this in two ways. First, illiteracy (both literal and political) is the product of politics, and second, in "as is the very literacy through which we try to overcome illiteracy," the very terms upon which "literacy" has meaning are themselves political. In other words, "literacy"—what it means to be able to "read"—is something defined on political terms.

It seems like being able to read or not is a fairly straightforward matter, more subtle questions of "functional illiteracy" (where one can read the words but not extract their meaning) aside. Not so for Freire. There's being able to read a text, and there's being able to read a society and its conditions, for Freire. Being able to read words on a page but failing to see how they, and the ability or inability to read them, maintain an oppressive state in society is another form of illiteracy (it is sometimes called "hermeneutical injustice" today). Being able to read the society as such but not being able to read words adequately to convince those in power that you know what you're experiencing ("testimonial injustice") is another meaning of being unjustly deemed unable to "read," or, at least, unable to "speak" what has been read.

As we can see, for Freire, being able to "read" bleeds over into what it means to be a "knower," someone who knows—or what it takes to *be considered* a knower, which is again understood as a political circumstance. He insists that the existing system (of society, education, literacy, etc.) regards literates as knowledgeable, even though this knowledge might be quite empty and useful only in participating and maintaining the existing oppressive conditions. On the other hand, "illiterates" are perceived as "absolutely ignorant," as people who do not know, but Freire says this ignores the fact that they know the contents of their lives. They know things, know they know things, and can be taught to "read" them. They are just denied the proper (that is, Marxist) context to understand the experiences of their lives, including why they are considered "illiterates," people who do not know and therefore are alienated from the process of transforming history and society.

> Illiterates know they are concrete men. They know that they do things. What they do not know in the culture of silence—in which they are ambiguous, dual beings—is that men's actions as such are transforming, creative, and re-creative. Overcome by the myths of this culture, including the myth of their own "natural inferiority," they do not know that *their* action upon the world is also transforming. Prevented from having a "structural perception" of the facts involving them, they do not know that they cannot "have a voice," that is, that they cannot exercise the right to participate consciously in the sociohistorical transformation of their society, because their work does not belong to them. (*The Politics of Education*, p. 50)

Of course, we see here Freire repeating the central contention of Marx: those oppressed by the existing system have their very humanity, as an extension of their work, stolen from them. This "unjust social reality," for Freire, is political in a multitude of ways at once, but primarily in the sense always meant by Marxists when discussing "political economy." The true nature of Man is that he is a maker of History, says Marx, a process from which the underclass is excluded by structural oppression and estrangement from their true nature as such. Freire sees this creative process as downstream from being regarded as a *knower*, and it is just a bourgeois conceit and matter of politicized definitions of "knowledge," "knowing," "knower," "literacy," "reading," "education," and so on that prevent the "illiterate" from realizing their true nature. Now we'll revisit some of Freire's words with greater context added,

> Learning to read and write ought to he an opportunity for men to know what *speaking the word* really means: a human act implying reflection and action. As such it is a primordial human right and not the privilege of a few. Speaking the word is not a true act if it is not at the same time associated with the right of self-expression and world-expression, of creating and re-creating, of deciding and choosing and ultimately participating in society's historical process.
>
> In the culture of silence the masses are mute, that is, they are prohibited from creatively taking part in the transformations of their society and therefore prohibited from being. Even if they can occasionally read and write because they were "taught" in human-itarian—but not humanist—literacy campaigns, they are never-theless alienated from the power responsible for their silence. (*The Politics of Education*, p. 50)

Notice that Freire reiterates yet again that learning to read and write in the *literal* sense isn't what he is interested in or talking about. Maybe people can "occasionally read or write because they were 'taught' in" the wrong kinds of literacy campaigns, which do not focus upon "political literacy" and condition them to accept allegedly dehuman-izing conditions. That doesn't really count, though, because it doesn't teach them to be true creators of history who know themselves as such. What we see Freire constructing here is a Marxist Theory of knowing, literacy, and education. Literally.

> In the banking concept of education, knowledge is a gift bestowed by those who consider themselves knowledgeable upon those whom they consider to know nothing. Projecting an absolute ignorance onto oth-ers, a characteristic of the ideology of oppression, negates education

and knowledge as processes of inquiry. The teacher presents himself to his students as their necessary opposite; by considering their ignorance absolute, he justifies his own existence. The students, alienated like the slave in the Hegelian dialectic, accept their ignorance as justifying the teachers existence—but, unlike the slave, they never discover that they educate the teacher. (*Pedagogy of the Oppressed*, p. 72)

"Knowledge is a gift bestowed by those who consider themselves knowledgeable upon those they consider to know nothing" *is* a Marxist Theory of knowing.

In the contemporary "Social Justice" epistemology literature, virtually all of which is framed in terms of education theory, this entire line of thinking is often characterized as the "knowing field," which is characterized as being "unlevel" and "silencing" those not privileged as knowers (say, by Kristie Dotson). The essential argument is that in various ways, the existing social order is biased and unjust because it favors certain "knowledges" and "ways of knowing" over others, which is considered to be effectively wholly political. Encountering this literature can be extremely disorienting, especially if one is unfamiliar with the Freirean Marxification of knowledge (and education).

The Marxification of Education

Being educated—we commonly hear "formally educated" from activists today—is framed out in Freirean thought as a form of bourgeois private property that is only accessible to certain elites who created that status and granted access to themselves and those they select. It is otherwise exclusive of others and "other ways of knowing." What society currently regards as "education," to Freire, is therefore a process of social and political grooming into maintaining the existing elite class, either by grooming its next generation of oppressors or by conditioning its next generation of oppressed to accept the terms of the existing society. This creates an oppressive social structure between the educated and uneducated that is established by that upper caste to benefit themselves and imposed upon the lower, putting them intrinsically in class conflict across the educated/illiterate line. The goal of a genuine education for Freire, then, is the awakening of the critical consciousness of this state of affairs in the underclass together with their own revolutionary consciousness by which they will eventually overthrow the unjust system. Everything else is false education that should be replaced by his own (Marxian) methods.

This bears a moment's elaboration in terms of its practical impacts. *All* effective pedagogies—which are never cited by Freire—are framed as the enabling part of the problem plaguing all of society, which is oppression. They're instruments of what Marxists would call "ideology," which is the term Marx used for the web of social myths and justifications the bourgeoisie offer to themselves and the rest of society for why they get to occupy positions of privilege. "Formal education" exists to allow some people, but not others, able to succeed in the prevailing system while failing and silencing everyone else, as Freire sees it, just as capital exists to keep a small elite successful in a market economy according to Marx. It exists to give those elites a justification for their success while inscribing on society the very terms that make their success false and oppressive. In other words, Freire is effectively insisting that all education other than his own approach is a rigged game meant to keep marginalized people "illiterate" where it matters, which is in terms of their "political literacy" and Marxist "conscientization."

Specifically, teaching someone to read so that they can get a good job, for Freire, merely enables them to participate in the existing system, which is bad. Not only is this a bourgeois conceit that ignores the plight of the oppressed, it also validates and reproduces the existing system itself, which in turn maintains or even concentrates the oppression of the illiterate by this structural arrangement of society. Education is sold to the underclass as a means of possibly joining the overclass, which, while failing most of them, provides a pathway for some of them to betray the class from which they came by abandoning it and helping maintain and justify the very system that causes the oppression in the first place. Thus, teaching people to read (or do math, etc.) is of low priority, as that is bourgeois knowledge not oriented toward political change, and subjects such as reading, mathematics, and everything else are better transformed into vehicles for a different kind of education with different priorities and goals. Specifically, learning skills valuable to existing social, political, and economic system is of minimal priority, if it is not intentionally avoided or disrupted. Instead, using existing subjects to generate Marxist political literacy and critical consciousness is advocated as primary. This is a *Marxist* Theory of being educated, and it is what Freirean pedagogy really is.

Both Freire and Marx are abundantly clear in what the purpose of their philosophical (read: theological) program is: the humanization of man, society, and the world (by making it Socialist). For Marx, the idea is that Man has to be led to recollect his true self, which he has been estranged from through the division of labor. That true self is a truly Social, or Socialist, Man who completely transcends the very idea of private property and private landholding and therefore undoes the division of labor (Fall of Man). Through his authentic work— with a hammer and sickle—he transforms the world into a garden, himself into a Socialist, and Society into a true Social Society, which is classless and stateless, freeing him up to go on garden-building free from any want, need, or demand of nature or others upon him. (Marx even says that working to satisfy a hungry belly is compelled work and thus not true, free work befitting men!) He is to *humanize* himself and his world by working to recollect his true *human* nature (as a "species-being," i.e., an individual who always works in the benefit of the species and those others within it, consciously). Freire imports this mysticism of what it means to be human directly into education and places it, instead of in actual work with a hammer and sickle, in education and knowing.

Humanizing Education

As we discussed at the end of the last chapter, Freire argues at length (particularly at the opening of chapter 6 of *The Politics of Education*) that all education is intrinsically political education because all education assumes a theory of Man and thus a politically relevant understanding of his relationship to Society. Education therefore either politicizes people into the standards of the existing society or into the (Marxist) liberation from it. There is no neutrality in education, then, to Freire. It's always political, either working to reproduce the allegedly dehumanizing society or teaching learners to denounce and replace it.

True education, Freire insists, has little to do with learning to read "disconnected symbols" or "memorizing" irrelevant simple sentences, like "Ava saw a grape" (English speakers might see this sample sentence in a similar light as "See Dick run") and should instead educate "learners" (no longer "students") in the context of their lives and the political ramifications of that context. These are to be interpreted by the "educator" (no longer "teacher") through a Marxist lens of class antagonism with the goal of awakening class consciousness. Not to put too fine a point on it, but chapter 8 of *The Politics of Education* bears the title "the process of political literacy" and describes exactly that. This process is carried out through the three methodological points referenced previously, most immediately, the utilization of "generative" words and concepts to awaken political literacy.

Marx described this program of awakening and then acting in accordance with his Theory as fundamentally *humanizing*. For Marx, what makes Man, Man, is that he is a conscious subject who can envision that which he wants to create, create it in the objective world, and then see himself as its creator in the thing he produced. In other words, he makes the world (and himself) more human—more suited to humanity and also more of a reflection of the human mind. Animals, while active and changing their environments, cannot do this. This is what makes Man uniquely human. Man can *transform the world* to make it more suited to himself and even like himself, whereas animals must accord themselves to the world. Indeed, he can do this *to himself* as well and thus recollect what it means to be truly human, which is to be a perfectly "social" Communist who has transcended the very idea of private property and the division of labor.

Therefore, the process of changing the objective world according to the subjective vision of Man is *humanizing* that object—making it more human through the subject-object dialectic at the heart of the Marxian theology. For Marx, Man doesn't only humanize the world, but through his productive work (hammer and sickle) he also humanizes himself by realizing himself to be a creative subject. He also works on his society when socially conscious ("Socialist Man"), thus humanizing Society and, in turn, the Man who lives in that society and is deterministically produced by its social relations (the inversion of praxis).

It's no coincidence that Freire describes his Critical Pedagogical approach as "humanistic education," which is the title of the ninth chapter of *The Politics of Education*. Freire insists this approach to education humanizes, or "hominizes," him (*hominização*)—literally makes him human, as if for the first time, rising up out of the animal world. Humanizing Man allows him to be in his true nature as a knower who can "speak the word to transform the world" into an even more hominized form. Animals cannot do this; it is what makes Man uniquely human.

> [M]en's relationships with the world are *per se* historical, as are men themselves. Not only do men make the history that makes them, but they can recount the history of this mutual making. In becoming "hominized" in the process of evolution, men become capable of

having a biography. Animals, on the contrary, are immersed in a time that belongs not to them but to men. (*The Politics of Education*, p. 71)[13]

The work that humanizes Man and the world, for Freire, arises from applying correct knowledge (in praxis), which comes from correct political education by which man can learn to see himself as a knower and transformer of History who can then take revolutionary action to actualize that in the world (and see himself as the one who did it). By seizing control of the production of knowledge (and education and literacy) to ensure its political relevance and context under Marxist assumptions, Freire's pedagogy aims to seize control of the development of Man and Society for "humanizing" ends. It's just a reproduction of Marxism. As Freire explains,

> For men, as beings of praxis, to transform the world is to humanize it, even if making the world human may not yet signify the humanization of men. It may simply mean impregnating the world with man's curious and inventive presence, imprinting it with the trace of his works. The process of transforming the world, which reveals this presence of man, can lead to his humanization as well as his dehumanization, to his growth or diminution. These alternatives reveal to man his problematic nature and pose a problem for him, requiring that he choose one path or the other. Often this very process of transformation ensnares man and his freedom to choose. Nevertheless, because they impregnate the world with

---

13 Incidentally, Freire quotes Marx, from *Capital*, on exactly this same point in the next paragraph: "There is a further fundamental distinction between man's relationships with the world and the animal's contacts with it: only men work. A horse, for example, lacks what is proper to man, what Marx refers to in his example of the bees: 'At the end of every labor-process, we get a result that already existed in the imagination of the laborer at its commencement.'"

their reflective presence, only men can humanize or dehumanize. Humanization is their utopia, which they announce in denouncing dehumanizing processes. (*The Politics of Education*, p. 70)

Freire waxes on this topic extensively—it is no mere sideshow to his program. Always it reproduces the Marxist *theology* at the heart of his worldview and project.

Dehumanization is a concrete expression of alienation and domination: humanistic education is a utopian project of the dominated and oppressed. Obviously both imply action by people in a social reality—the first, in the sense of preserving the status quo, the second in a radical transformation of the oppressor's world.

It seems important here to emphasize what is most obvious—the interrelationship of dehumanization and humanistic education. Again, both require action from men and women to maintain or modify their respective realities. We emphasize this to overcome idealist illusions and pipe dreams of an eventual humanistic education for mankind without the necessary transformation of an oppressed and unjust world. Such a dream actually serves the interests of the advantaged and readily exposes an ideology that concretizes the welfare syndrome by urging the oppressed to wait patiently for those sunnier days, delayed for now, but soon to appear. (*The Politics of Education*, p. 114)

There, in fact, Freire effectively reproduces in other language Marx's famous articulation of religion as the "opium of the people," a kind of numbing agent that makes one's suffering bearable instead of an impetus for change. Here's how Marx put that in his 1844 "Contribution to the Critique of Hegel's *Philosophy of Right*,"

Religious suffering is, at one and the same time, the expression of real suffering and a protest against real suffering. Religion is the sigh of the oppressed creature, the heart of a heartless world, and the soul of soulless conditions. It is the opium of the people.

The abolition of religion as the illusory happiness of the people is the demand for their real happiness. To call on them to give up their illusions about their condition is to call on them to give up a condition that requires illusions. (p. I)

Freire's objective in invoking this view of the world is clear; it's to make the case that his understanding of the purpose of education is the only possible legitimate one:

In truth, there is no humanization without liberation, just as there is no liberation without a revolutionary transformation of the class society, for in the class society all humanization is impossible. Liberation becomes concrete only when society is changed, not when its structures are simply modernized. (*The Politics of Education*, p. I36)

The process, for Freire, is equally clear: Man must take (Marxist) action to free himself from his oppressive conditions, just like the mostly illiterate and innumerate children laying on the statehouse steps in Providence, Rhode Island.

In the light of such a concept—unfortunately, all too widespread—literacy programs can never be efforts toward freedom; they will never question the very reality that deprives men of the right to speak up—not only illiterates but all those who are treated as objects in a dependent relationship. These men, illiterate or not, are in fact not marginal. What we said before bears repeating: They are not "beings outside of"; they are "beings for another." Therefore the solution to their problem is to become, not "beings inside of," but men freeing themselves; for, in reality, they are not marginal to the structure, but oppressed men within it. Alienated men, they cannot overcome their dependency by "incorporation" into the very structure responsible for their dependency. There is no other road to humanization—theirs as well as everyone else's—other than authentic transformation of the dehumanizing structure. (*The Politics of Education*, pp. 48–49)

This is what the academically cheated students of Providence understand implicitly, even if they've never heard of any of these people or ideas directly: the world as it is, is dehumanizing, and nothing within that world means much of anything other than denouncing and transforming the structure they've been taught to see as dehumanizing. Regular literacy, Freire explains, here and in the paragraphs that follow, *will not do* for this. Neither would math, history, or any other subject taught *except as a "mediator" to political knowledge*. Genuine education would merely reinsert people into the society in which they are made "beings for another." The only way out is Marxism, the allegedly only "scientific" study of their situation.

For this very reason, denunciation and annunciation in this utopian pedagogy are not meant to be empty words, but an historic [sic] commitment. Denunciation of a dehumanizing situation today increasingly demands precise scientific understanding of that situation. Similarly, the annunciation of its transformation increasingly requires a theory of transforming action. Yet, neither act by itself implies the transformation of the denounced reality or the establishment of that which is announced. Rather, as a moment in a historical process, the announced reality is already present in the act of denunciation and annunciation. (*The Politics of Education*, p. 57)

This is the education system that has been brought to our kids because our kids, like the kids in Providence, now go to Paulo Freire's schools. It is a Marxified educational program (thought reform) that teaches our kids that they are trapped in a dehumanizing system and only through Marxist consciousness and activism can they hope to escape it—and set everyone else free in the process. Reading, writing, mathematics, science, history are all cast to the side in the quest for "humanization."

Formal Education as Domestication

So, Freire sees the awakening of political consciousness through his own methods to be uniquely humanizing. Other forms of education are "dehumanizing" or reproduce "dehumanizing" structures. "Learners" are no longer learning to reproduce (as students) the ideas and knowledge of the corrupt society that has marginalized them. They are active, creative subjects in their own educational process.

> If learning to read and write is to constitute an act of knowing, the learners must assume from the beginning the role of creative subjects. It is not a matter of memorizing and repeating given syllables, words, and phrases, but rather of reflecting critically on the process of reading and writing itself, and on the profound significance of language. (*The Politics of Education*, pp. 49–50)

Learners in a Freirean political education program come to see themselves as creative subjects involved in their own process of learning (production and creation), whereas those being taught as students are objectified and alienated, just like Marx would say, by being taught someone else's knowledge. (Marx said alienation arises when workers are made or paid to do work consistent with the subjective vision in someone else's head rather than that in their own.) Recall, however, that the entire Marxist concept of man and the world depends upon separating that which is *human* from that which is *animal* (and, for completeness, that which is machine). Thus, the dichotomy Freire offers is between a "humanizing" or "liberating" education (his) and any other is equivalent to choosing between a "domesticating" and "humanizing" one. Education can make you more like a fully conscious human being (that is, a dialectical entity) or render you non-dialectical and therefore like a (domesticated) animal.

Through improper education, then, students come to see themselves as functional members or washouts of a society they do not realize is actually domesticating them to the will of the powerful elites. Through a proper (Freirean) political education program, however, learners come to see themselves as learners who are both in the world and with it, in a position to transform it out of that condition and into a worldly Kingdom. (Christian readers will shudder here again, as Christ commands to be in the world but not of it.)

> The starting point for such an analysis must be a critical comprehension of man as a being who exists *in* and *with* the world. Since the basic condition for conscientization is that its agent must be a subject (i.e., a conscious being), conscientization, like education, is specifically and exclusively a human process. It is as conscious beings that men are not only *in* the world but *with* the world, together with other men. Only men, as "open" beings, are able to achieve the complex operation of simultaneously transforming the world by their action and grasping and expressing the world's reality in their creative language. (*The Politics of Education*, p. 68)

Outside of Freire's program, education "domesticates" learners to stay complacent and non-revolutionary, trapping them in a "culture of silence." It stabilizes them and gives them the opportunity to capitalize upon what they learn in the existing system, thus upholding it, and this, in turn, provides a good, stable life that leads them not only to reject revolutionary radicalism but also to actively resist it as a counter-revolutionary, at least to echo the most influential Critical Marxist, Herbert Marcuse, on the point:

> By virtue of its basic position in the production process, by virtue of its numerical weight and the weight of exploitation, the working class is still the historical agent of revolution; by virtue of its sharing the stabilizing needs of the system, it has become a conservative, even counterrevolutionary force. Objectively, "in-itself," labor still is the potentially revolutionary class; subjectively, "for-itself," it is not. (*An Essay on Liberation*, p. 16)

In fact, actual education is a worse state of affairs for Freire because education enables oppressed people to turn around and become oppressors instead of becoming revolutionaries because they haven't thrown off the underlying logic of a class-based society. (This is a Critical Marxist Theory of education, by the way—the Marcusian analogue would be the desire to rise up the ladder and become a manager or setter of culture.) Becoming educated therefore leads them to reproduce that society and the oppression that defines it, which, following Marx, Freire characterizes as intrinsically *dehumanizing*.

> But almost always, during the initial stage of the struggle, the oppressed, instead of striving for liberation, tend themselves to become oppressors, or "sub-oppressors." The very structure of their thought has been conditioned by the contradictions of the concrete, existential situation by which they were shaped. Their ideal is to be men; but for them, to be men is to be oppressors. This is their model of humanity. This phenomenon derives from the fact that the oppressed, at a certain moment of their existential experience, adopt an attitude of "adhesion" to the oppressor. ... In this situation the oppressed do not see the "new man" as the person to be

born from the resolution of this contradiction, as oppression gives way to liberation. For them, the new man or woman themselves become oppressors. Their vision of the new man or woman is individualistic; because of their identification with the oppressor, they have no consciousness of themselves as persons or as members of an oppressed class. It is not to become free that they want agrarian reform, but in order to acquire land and thus become landowners— or, more precisely, bosses over other workers. (*Pedagogy of the Oppressed*, pp. 45–46)

Alternatively, education fails for the peasant because it isn't relevant to him or because it convinces him the operating logic of the world is "just the way it is." This failure dulls the learner into accepting his fate, inducing him into a fatalistic acceptance of his own "culture of silence" in which he doesn't have the language or other "epistemic resources" (in later Critical Pedagogy literature) to speak or be heard. He may be literate, but he cannot actually read or speak, as Freire would have it, because he hasn't been conscientized or taught political literacy. Instead, he's been domesticated by the prevailing social order, often through education that fails to be "humanizing."

By the way, these ideas haven't been idle in the philosophy of education academic literature. The contemporary concepts of "epistemic injustice," "epistemic oppression," and "epistemic violence" promulgated by Social Justice scholars like Miranda Fricker, Kristie Dotson, and their followers echo these Freirean concepts. It's mainstream Woke Marxist thought in education that without a radical political education put forth on their terms, certain "learners" and "knowers" are marginalized and domesticated by the existing knowledge and education systems while others are privileged.

Indeed, Fricker's ideas of "testimonial injustice" (the testimony of marginalized "knowers" isn't deemed credible) and "hermeneutic injustice" (marginalized "knowers" lack the accepted epistemic resources to communicate their ideas on acceptable terms to dominant "knowers" and are thus ignored) are incredibly similar to Freire's. Dotson extended Fricker's account into a complete three-dimensional theory of "epistemic oppression" (by adding an "irreducible" form that is the product of what is considered "knowing" within a given system itself), all focused on how it silences those oppressed by it. This could be seen as a rewrite of the "problem of reproduction" that Critical Pedagogy stepped onto the scene to solve. For Freire, a humanizing education into conscientization is the only way to break this "culture of silence." For these later Theorists, it is typically framed in terms of "leveling the unlevel knowing field."[14]

"Leveling the knowing field" is, then, ultimately the point of a Freirean Marxified education, where by "leveling" we understand it to mean "tilting it to Marxist advantage." The Marxification of education, ultimately, is little more than a repackaging of basic Marxist beliefs into the domain of education, whether by intention or not. In place of capital, there is literacy, being educated, and being regarded as a knower. The advantaged class in society establishes these statuses to privilege some and marginalize others. It does this to keep advantaging itself and to convince itself it deserves this advantage. Those outside of that circumstance, together with some within it, need to be awakened to this unjust organization of society and act to reorganize

---

14 These ideas from Fricker and Dotson, both highly influential critical education Theorists, are merely mentioned here without much elaboration to give the reader a sense that these ideas have been developed and applied considerably since Freire's earlier formulations. So pervasive have been Freire's ideas that neither Fricker nor Dotson mention him while recreating the key ideas from his Marxist Theory of Knowledge, whether by intention, oversight, or because they just became the air that scholars by the early 2000s and 2010s were breathing. For more detail on these ideas in an accessible way that relates them to the postmodern Theory they do reference, readers are encouraged to study the eighth chapter of *Cynical Theories* (2020, Pluckrose and Lindsay).

it for "justice." This "justice" will be achieved by those conscientized to the "true nature of reality" denouncing the existing society so that a new society can emerge. Doing this requires seizing the means of the production of knowledge and education to produce political knowledge on Marxist terms so that learners can be conscientized. This is Paulo Freire's Marxification of Education, and its purpose is to create the preconditions for what Marxists call "liberation," not an educated populace.

IV.

PREPARING THE CULTURAL REVOLUTION

Having established *what* Freirean education is, we're going to begin
to transition into *why* it is employed and then *how* it works (insofar
as it does work, i.e., for conscientization). We'll begin by clarifying
that Freire sees education as an intrinsically political phenomenon
upon which one must take a side. This framing isn't a mere question
of values, as discussed previously, but a question of the entire concept of man and the world that inform values-driven education. For
Freire, there is only one legitimate side: Dialectical Leftism, which he
equates with the pursuit of liberation through his own Marxist methods. Thus, for Freire, there is only one purpose to education, which is
establishing the preconditions for a bid for liberation through Critical
Marxist cultural revolution.

Education, as we usually think of it, is to Freire nothing better than a process of social domestication that must be rejected and
replaced with his own program of cultural revolution for liberation.
In education as it is, all one learns is how to reproduce the world or
to accept it on terms set by someone else. In his approach, however,
one learns to speak the word (to proclaim the world) by learning to
reject the intrinsically oppressive logic of existing society. Education
reinforces oppression and the imposed "culture of silence" on society's undesirables. Freirean pedagogy breaks that "culture of silence"
and allows marginalized "concrete" knowers to express themselves
politically in a (Marxist) transformative way. Freire indicates this is

necessary in place of other educational approaches specifically in order to fulfill exactly what Marx laid out: to become a historical (meaning History-making) subject. To repeat a few key quotations again for clarity and emphasis,

> In the culture of silence the masses are mute, that is, they are prohibited from creatively taking part in the transformations of their society and therefore prohibited from being. Even if they can occasionally read and write because they were "taught" in humanitarian—but not humanist—literacy campaigns, they are nevertheless alienated from the power responsible for their silence. (*The Politics of Education*, p. 50)

The goal of such a subject is to restore himself to true being by realizing himself to be a transformer (that is, creator) of History. The role of such a subject is to seize control of the means of production—material, cultural, or whatever is "making man" in the given context—and shaping the evolution of the ever-emerging New Society:

> Learning to read and write ought to be an opportunity for men to know what *speaking the word* really means: a human act implying reflection and action. As such it is a primordial human right and not the privilege of a few. Speaking the word is not a true act if it is not at the same time associated with the right of self-expression and world-expression, of creating and re-creating, of deciding and choosing and ultimately participating in society's historical process. (*The Politics of Education*, p. 50)

To the initiated, the Marxism isn't even trying to hide in Freire's discussion of what humanization means or how it is achieved through this conscientization, which we'll look at in greater depth in the next chapter. Neither is the *Marxification* of educational theory itself, which replaces actual education with this "humanizing" process.

> Instead of being an alienating transference of knowledge, education or cultural action for freedom is the authentication of knowledge by which learners and educators as "consciousness" or as ones filled with "intention" join in the quest for new knowledge as a consequence of their apprehending existing knowledge. But, again, if education as a practice of freedom is to achieve this understanding of existing knowledge in the search for new knowledge, it can never do so by "treating" consciousness in the same way dominating education "treats" it. The educator who makes a humanistic choice must correctly perceive the relationship between consciousness and world, and man and world. A liberating form of educational practice by definition proposes an "archaeology" of consciousness. Through their own efforts people can remake the natural path where consciousness emerges as the capacity for self-perception. In the act of *hominização* [humanization, becoming human], in which reflection establishes itself, one sees the "individual and instantaneous leap from instinct to thought." This is so because at that very remote moment the reflective consciousness characterized a human as an animal capable not only of knowing but also of knowing himself or herself in the process of knowing. Thus, consciousness emerges as "intention" and not just as a receptacle to be filled. (*The Politics of Education*, p. 115)

Just like how Marx said to be human is to be able to be conscious of being conscious, Freire sees it as being able to know (that is, be conscious of) yourself as a knower in the process of knowing (that is, of being conscious). Thus, for both Marx and Freire, Man is a consciously knowing subject who can know that he is that and able to act from that consciousness—and this is what makes him human.

The stratification of society, ultimately through the division of labor and class status, alienates Man from himself by preventing him from being able to do these things or to know that he could do these things under the right conditions. Thus, he's not allowed to *be* because he's not allowed to *become* what he really is (a Communist who lives in a to-be-realized Communist Utopia).

Freire frames this distinction between domesticating and humanizing education—that is, anything-but-his versus his model of education—in terms of that which generates intention-driven consciousness and that which doesn't. Readers familiar with what's happening in education will, of course, recognize this particular word, *intention*. Now they will realize that the otherwise strange word "intentional" that appears in so much education literature and practice refers to a Marxist root.

> In its relation to consciousness and world, education as a dominating task assumes that consciousness is and should be merely an empty receptacle to be "filled"; education as a liberating and humanistic task views consciousness as "intention" toward the world. (*The Politics of Education*, p. 114)

Of course, that "'intention' toward the world" is the intention to transform it into a Marxist "Utopia,"[15] as Freire states repeatedly throughout all of his works. So here Freire makes his intentions

---

15 Marx, some will note, was explicitly against utopianism, but this is mostly another intellectual or linguistic swindle on his part. By saying he's against utopianism while describing the final state of Society and Man as existing in a utopian condition, all he's saying is that the perfected society (the Utopia) can be realized and thus isn't technically a Utopia, which literally means "No-place," i.e., outside of the realm of the possible. Marcuse and Freire, with Giroux behind him, explicitly reclaim the term for the eventual society for which they advocate, however.

completely explicit. If you actually educate students, you are engaging in a "dominating task." On the other hand, if you want to "liberate" and "humanize" them, you have to groom them into an "intention" toward remaking the world by applying Marxist analysis and activism to generate a perpetual cultural revolution—no exaggeration. In the Marxist (thus Freirean) view, consciousness itself has an intention of transformation and humanization, you see, and genuine education suppresses that by obscuring the "real conditions" of the world from students.

> Banking education inhibits creativity and domesticates (although it cannot completely destroy) the *intentionality* of consciousness by isolating consciousness from the world, thereby denying people their ontological and historical vocation of becoming more fully human. (*Pedagogy of the Oppressed*, pp. 83–84)

Again, note well that while Freire specifies *banking education* here, which seems mostly to exaggerate and criticize the Prussian model, it implicates all pedagogical approaches other than his. For those reading these remarks and thinking, "yeah, that's kind of true, though," because on the Prussian model it can tend in that direction, recognize that other methods of education than the Prussian model are possible, as is genuine education that is neither Freirean nor "banking." Freire creates a false choice between "banking" education and "dialogical" education by insisting anywhere there is a dynamic where the teacher is in some way more knowledgeable than the students (or, indeed, that a hierarchical teacher/student model is employed), it is necessarily *not dialogical* and thus "banking" education.

Nonetheless, it's now very obvious why students who would attend a school based in Freirean Critical Pedagogy would be far less likely to achieve academic mastery of any subject. Despite claims that his approach is a vehicle to subject mastery, it's simply not the point.

Neither is it the point in derivative modes of education that follow from the Freirean method, like Culturally Relevant Teaching and Social-Emotional Learning, whatever lip-service they pay to academic achievement. It's also obvious why products of these programs would be far more likely to become know-nothing activists who think everything in the world is extremely problematic and in need of radical transformation than educated, productive citizens. Making them into activists *is* the point. This is what you get when your kids go to Paulo Freire's schools.

Freire's Critical Utopianism

So how is one to know if he is participating in a Freirean educational approach, and what does it end up entailing? In addition to the hallmark techniques and approaches described further below, especially including the "dialogical" model just mentioned, two primary criteria are offered by Freire. One, the approach must be *utopian*. Two, in being utopian, it must use the appropriate *critical* disposition and method, which technically defines it as being utopian. Of note, Freire identifies *utopianism* as the defining characteristic of the Left and *impossible* for the Right, by definition. Indeed, it is the defining characteristic of the *Dialectical Left* that is ultimately committed to the Marxist vision of transforming society into its dream of a perfected stateless, classless global community.

Utopianism, for Freire, begins with a particular attitudinal disposition: Leftist Scientific Gnosticism, i.e., a peculiar religious disposition, both generally and in terms of Establishment Clause jurisprudence.

> The process of writing on a particular theme is not just a narrative act. In perceiving the theme as a phenomenon that takes place in a concrete reality and that mediates men and women, we writers must assume a gnosiological attitude. ... Our committed, but nonneutral

attitude toward the reality we are trying to know must first render knowledge as a process involving an action and reflection of man in the world. By virtue of the teleological character in the unity of action and reflection (that is, of praxis), by which a man or woman who transforms the world is transformed, he or she cannot discard this attitude of commitment that, in turn, preserves his or her critical spirit and scientism. We cannot remain ethically indifferent to the fate that may be imposed on our findings by those who have the power of decisions, but merely yield to science and its interests and subsequently dictate their aims to the majority. (*The Politics of Education*, p. 112)

What this means is that a Freirean educational approach must adopt and communicate the underlying Marxist machinery, themes, purpose, and ideology in service of the Marxist goal of seizing the means of production of the society (thus man and the world) and transforming the world accordingly (humanizing it). Astute readers will recognize that Freire says this requires a *gnosiological* attitude, which is what Marxists often call their theory of knowledge. (Christians will again shudder as they realize this indicates that Marxism is ultimately a Gnostic heresy running within a diabolical man-as-gods software routine.)

In Woke Marxism, accepting "other ways of knowing," so long as those are rooted in the broad Critical Theory method and its intrinsic "teleological character" (expression of some ultimate purpose), is that "gnosiological" attitude—one that preserves his critical spirit and scientism (religious faith in what gets passed off as "science"). It claims to arise from a glimpse of absolute knowledge (*gnosis*) of the reality of Man and Society, which it posits lies in the lived experience of oppression. (Marx saw this glimpse of reality as existing in the phenomenological "fact" of suffering due to the structural aspects of reality.) For Freire, and thus the Woke Marxists, we must do this because the illiterate, by virtue of the "realities" of their lives and marginalization through illiteracy, are in fact already knowers in possession of a more important and unrecognized (excluded) knowledge that's needed to correctly transform the world. They're "concrete men" who "know" and "know that they do things," but they're excluded from knowing the "concrete realities" of their "structural conditions" without a proper (Freirean) political education. We will return to this theme in the next chapter as this "knowledge" is made concrete and actionable, for Freire, through the process of conscientization—another (neo)-Marxist concept at the heart of his whole educational program.

To be clear, it isn't that Freire *just* Marxified education and that it doesn't include Marxist indoctrination as well. Freire unapologetically uses his Marxified educational theory (Critical Pedagogy) to teach a Critical variation of Marxist Theory, too. He is absolutely clear (and devotes chapters of his books) to the objective of his educational program: to raise a Marxist or critical consciousness in "learners" so that they might engage in revolutionary struggle to overthrow the existing system. The underlying (neo)-Marxist ideology is obvious throughout his writing, tinged as it is with radical postcolonialism. In fact, Freire argues clearly in *The Politics of Education* that following the revolution, if achieved, the need for a critical consciousness and critical education theory to facilitate it *increases* rather than resolves itself. The New Society, even as it emerges, you see, is already the right-wing of the ongoing transformational process; it's the new "status quo." He then goes on to explain that the revolution must be *perpetual* to be authentic so that it never becomes a (necrophiliac, "death loving") status quo, which will be imposed upon everyone by the power-elites who benefit from it.

This attitude, however, is one allegedly filled with hope because it is a *process of liberation*. Education exists to lead students into this appropriate "scientific understanding" of the conditions of their lives and the appropriate "gnosiological attitude" for interpreting it in an ongoing process of Leftism. It is also purposed: to bring about the utopian condition. It also has a method, through relentless "denunciation and annunciation," which is the distillation of the Critical Marxist project famously known as "Critical Theory." Critical Theory can only be correctly applied from that "gnosiological attitude" and a "historic commitment" to its transformational praxis.

A Radical New Hope

Freire didn't advocate for much *classical Marxism* through his program, however. He was a neo-Marxist and Liberation Theologian, both of which put him at odds with classical Marxists, who have, in their own right, criticized Freire viciously for these positions. Freire teaches a combined Critical Marxist Theory and Liberation Theology with his Marxified education model. In so doing, he particularly focuses on the neo-Marxist goal of conscientization (raising critical consciousness out of ideologically conditioned false consciousness or general lack of consciousness), which he frames in terms of the material and social conditions of the lives of the "oppressed." It is in this way that the terms of the existing society themselves are thrown off and the "new man" doesn't come to repeat the oppression he believes structures society by becoming another one of the bosses, landowners, ideologists, or bourgeoisie.

Thus, we see the strong turn to the phenomenological concept at the heart of much of Woke Marxism: "lived experience." His disposition toward Liberation Theology explains his appeals to hope (that Marxism will work this time) and love (epitomized, apparently, in Che Guevara) as well as the overtly religious character of his view of conscientization as the purpose of education.

Che Guevara is an example of the unceasing witness revolutionary leadership gives to dialogue with the people. The more we study his work, the more we perceive his conviction that anyone who wants to become a true revolutionary must be in "communion" with the people. Guevara did not hesitate to recognize the capacity to love as an indispensable condition for authentic revolutionaries. ... [Guevara] became a guerrilla not out of desperation but because, as a lover of men, he dreamt of a new man being born in the experience of liberation. In this sense, Guevara incarnated the authentic revolutionary utopia. He was one of the great prophets of the silent ones of the Third World. ... In citing Guevara and his witness as a guerrilla, we do not mean to say that revolutionaries elsewhere are obliged to repeat the same witness. What is essential is that they strive to achieve communion with the people as he did, patiently and unceasingly. Communion with the people—accessible only to those with a utopian vision, in the sense referred to in this essay—is one of the fundamental characteristics of cultural action for freedom. (*The Politics of Education*, p. 84)

The "utopian" process Freire recommends here is one of ceaselessly denouncing the existing world from a position of consciousness, which automatically announces the possibility of a new world when done *critically*, i.e., with Marxist consciousness—that gnosiological attitude. This will bring about an ideal world eventually as every wrong aspect of society is denounced, allowing the annunciation of new possibilities, which presumably will blossom over time (with Che Guevara as the idealized role model for the process). Again, this is little different than the vision of the Critical Marxist Herbert Marcuse, who wrote in 1969,

Negative thinking draws whatever force it may have from its empirical basis: the actual human condition in the given society, and the "given" possibilities to transcend this condition, to enlarge the realm of freedom. In this sense, negative thinking is by virtue of its own internal concepts "positive": oriented toward, and comprehending a

— 76 —

future which is "contained" in the present. And in this containment (which is an important aspect of the general containment policy pursued by the established societies), the future appears as possible liberation. It is not the only alternative: the advent of a long period of "civilized" barbarism, with or without the nuclear destruction, is equally contained in the present. Negative thinking, and the praxis guided by it, is the positive and positing effort to prevent this utter negativity. (*An Essay on Liberation*, p. 89)

Christians will, incidentally, shudder again, and not just from the Hermetic mystery religion expressed here. They'll shudder even more deeply should they look closely at what emerges from this view, Freirean "critical hope," which perverts the call to faith in Hebrews 11:1 almost perfectly, replacing faith in God with a call to Marxist activism.

There is no annunciation without denunciation, just as every denunciation generates annunciation. Without the latter, hope is impossible. In an authentic utopian vision, however, hoping does not mean folding one's arms and waiting. Waiting is only possible when one, filled with hope, seeks through reflective action to achieve that announced future which is being born within the denunciation.

That is why there is no genuine hope in those who intend to make the future repeat their present, or in those who see the future as something predetermined. Both have a domesticated notion of history: the former because they want to stop time, the latter because they are certain about a future they already "know." Utopian hope, on the contrary, is engagement full of risk. That is why the dominators, who merely denounce those who denounce them and have nothing to announce but the presentation of the status quo, can never be utopian or, for that matter, prophetic. (*The Politics of Education*, p. 58)

Hope, for Freire, lies in the fact that we can denounce the existing world and take action to disrupt and dismantle its processes and ways of knowing (so, Marcuse's "negative thinking"). Hope resides in the belief that we don't have to live with domestication through education and might one day arrive at a place in time when it comes to an end. So we read in Hebrews: "Now faith is confidence in what we hope for and assurance about what we do not see." The thing is, for Freire, we are not to know what the utopian future looks like. That would lead us to impose it, which is a right-wing error and a new form of oppression. We're merely to denounce from consciousness and engage in the Marxist praxis and... hope.

Clearly, the Freirean model is actually hopeless. That doesn't mean it doesn't do anything, nor does it mean it fails to provide hope for Dialectical Leftists who had all but given up. Consider how Henry Giroux comments on what Freire's pedagogy brought to Critical Marxism just as it was beginning to fail and falter in the 1970s, just as the "sixties radicals" were making their way, as Isaac Gottesman tells us, into the classrooms.

> For the new sociology of education, schools were analyzed primarily within the language of critique and domination. Since schools were viewed primarily as reproductive in nature, left critics failed to provide a programmatic discourse through which contrasting hegemonic practices could be established. The agony of the left in this case was that its language of critique offered no hope for teachers, parents, or students to wage a political struggle within the schools themselves. Consequently, the language of critique was subsumed within the discourse of despair. (*The Politics of Education*, pp. xv–xvi)

What brought hope back to the radicals is Freire's insistence that by changing ourselves—radical death and rebirth—and then taking action to denounce and announce, liberation from oppressive structures (on Marxist terms) might actually have a chance. The goal of his educational program, as he makes plain, is therefore *conscientization* (*conscientização*, in Freire's Brazilian Portuguese), and it's exceptionally effective and efficient at producing it. The *process* of political education, for Freire, is this: conscientization. What he means by it is quite literally the process of Marxist (or Maoist) thought reform.

So, if Freire's is allegedly a "pedagogy of hope," as the title to his semi-autobiographical 1992 book suggests, what is it hopeful for? Freire's answer is explicit, as we saw: perpetual cultural revolution. Put another way, this is a perpetual lack of that same stability Marcuse identified in 1969 as an intrinsically stabilizing force that robs the revolutionary class of its revolutionary potential. It is chaos as a ladder with rungs made out of your made-dysfunctional kids who have been programmed as activists who believe they simply cannot live in a world that isn't pointed toward a sustainable Marxian Utopia.

V.

CONSCIENTIZATION

Now we really come to the point. Conscientization is the chief *goal* of the Freirean educational program. It means bringing someone to Marxist consciousness of their circumstances. In the big picture, it proceeds by a broad method I'll refer to as "Freirean" that proceeds in three steps: (1) identifying the relevant context of the "learner" to discover "generative themes"; (2) presenting back to the learner images or other abstract representations of his context ("codifications") represented in the generative themes; and (3) problematization of those representations and the context they represent in the "learners'" lives ("decodification") to "conscientize" them to the "real conditions" of the "political context" of their lives. The Freirean process is supposed to teach literacy (or other academic mastery) on the back of this political literacy program that is said to properly engage "learners" in the learning process.[16]

The Freirean methodology, as we'll discuss in greater detail in the coming chapters, achieves these steps through dialogue and conversation between learners and "educators," who are seen as *facilitators*. That is, they facilitate Freire's hallmark "dialogical model" of education that replaces the "banking model." A "conscientized" learner will be *politically literate* and will therefore be able to recognize the "actual"

---

16 Freire, in an appendix to chapter 7 of *The Politics of Education*, insists that decodification takes place in five stages that culminate with what pretends to be the literacy lesson.

conditions of his life, their "structural" causes, and his role in changing them. Crucially, all of this will be understood from a perspective that sides with the "oppressed" or "the people" in solidarity with them (hence, the *pedagogy of the oppressed*). Conscientization, as we saw previously, is for Freire tantamount to a religious death and rebirth—indeed, the *true meaning of Easter*, which must be existentially experienced to be valid. That's clearly an undeniable religious conversion experience.

Conscientization Works But Does Not Educate

A more accurate presentation of this three-step process would be: (1) data-mining the students by one method or another to discover what might radicalize them; (2) presenting radicalizing material *through the established curriculum*; and (3) grooming students' responses to this material to ensure it radicalizes them into Marxist "critical consciousness." That is, it is a process of thought reform. Recall what the researchers investigating Freirean approach saw in Nigeria:

> **Stage Two: The Selection of Words from The Discovered Vocabulary**
> From the discussions of the learners, the Generative Words written by the team of facilitators were: resources, money, abundance, crude oil, stealing, pocket, begging, plenty, poverty, suffering, frustration, crying, hunger, crisis, dying, death.
>
> These words were later depicted in pictorial form showing the concrete realities and situations in the lives of the people. The pictorial display provoked an emotional state of pity and anger among the discussants, some of them could not talk, while most of them were moved to tears asking the question: Why! Why! Why! Why!

To avoid any confusion, note that what the researchers present as "Stage Two" encompasses much of what I called steps (2) and (3) above. What they call "Stage Three" is "the actual process of literacy training," which in a Freirean mode would be both literally learning to read and write and increased focus on "political literacy" in the contexts of their lives, as presented above. If you recall, however, their "learners" never got there. They turned into "emotional wrecks" and refused to learn to read at all.

Stage Three: The Actual Process of Literacy Training
After the completion of stage two, it came as a great surprise to the facilitators, that the discussants were not willing to participate in the literacy teaching/training process. They were in a state of emotional wreck. They were furious, angry, shouting and restless. They were shouting Change! Change! Change! Cursing furiously those who have, in one way or the other, contributed to the suffering of the people. The bottom-line: acquisition of basic literacy skills did not make any meaning to them and in fact was irrelevant, with some of them asking the facilitators:

"What have you people, who are learned, done to change the situation, rather you (have) worsened the situation when you yourself get to the position."

Conscientization therefore definitely *works*, as radicalization of "learners" is clearly achieved, but it not only fails to educate but also produces conditions under which education is virtually impossible—what, following Freire (below) might be called a "victim's mentality." Perhaps amusingly, Freire seemed to be aware of this problem from very early on, though it did not deter him. He even describes it in the preface to *Pedagogy of the Oppressed* before dismissing it as ridiculous (on preposterous Marxist terms) and blaming the system and people to whom it happens for its occurrence. To quote him on it at unfortunate length:

In one of these discussions, the group was debating whether the *conscientização* of men and women to a specific situation of injustice might not lead them to "destructive fanaticism" or to a "sensation of total collapse of their world." ...

Doubt regarding the possible effects of *conscientização* implies a premise which the doubter does not always make explicit: It is better for the victims of injustice not to recognize themselves as such. In fact, however, *conscientização* does not lead people to "destructive fanaticism." On the contrary, by making it possible for people to enter the historical process as responsible Subjects, *conscientização* enrolls them in the search for self-affirmation and thus avoids fanaticism,

> The awakening of critical consciousness leads the way to the expression of social discontents precisely because these discontents are real components of an oppressive situation.

Fear of freedom, of which its possessor is not necessarily aware, makes him see ghosts. Such an individual is actually taking refuge in an attempt to achieve security, which he or she prefers to the risks of liberty. As Hegel testifies:

> It is solely by risking life that freedom is obtained; ... the individual who has not staked his or her life may, no doubt, be recognized as a Person; but he or she has not attained the truth of this recognition as an independent self-consciousness.

Men and women rarely admit their fear of freedom openly, however, tending rather to camouflage it—sometimes unconsciously—by presenting themselves as defenders of freedom. They give their doubts and misgivings an air of profound sobriety, as befitting custodians of freedom. But they confuse freedom with the maintenance of the status quo; so that if *conscientização* threatens to place that status quo in question, it thereby seems to constitute a threat to freedom itself. (*Pedagogy of the Oppressed*, pp. 35–36)

Evidence disagrees with Freire, but Freire escapes evidence by constructing his pedagogy so as to blame failures on those implementing it or broken by it rather than on the method itself. Allow me to insist that this disastrous result is guaranteed, however, because, as Freire himself indicated, the actual literacy process—learning to read and write—is at best second in importance, if not irrelevant, to the actual ambitions of his method. Plainly, the goals of his educational method are raising "political literacy" and stimulating "learners" to activism. That is, the real point of Freirean pedagogy is conscientization, and in practice it renders actual literacy superfluous in those brainwashed by it. As we saw previously in a number of his own remarks, Freire makes this sufficiently clear himself.

To make it abundantly clear, the goal of Freire's process is not at all to get students to learn to read (or have other academic achievement) unless by happy accident. That's the sales pitch. That's the con. It is to get them to *recognize their political context* and their own roles as conscious participants in transforming it, in Marxist fashion, with the help of "educators" as facilitators in the process. The method is to *intentionally repurpose and misuse* existing academic curricula as vehicles for this process—killing them, gutting them, and wearing their skins as suits like a wolf in sheep's clothing. In that it steals education and achieves radicalization in its place, it definitely *works*, but it does not *educate*.

Conscientization as Thought Reform

There's another way to understand conscientization that is positively chilling and stubbornly difficult to discount once the connection is made. *Conscientização* is the process of *thought reform*, which is the translation psychologist Robert Jay Lifton gave to the Mandarin Chinese term for "brainwashing" in Maoist re-education prisons in Communist China (xǐnǎo, 洗脑). (Cult/political *grooming* would be another acceptable term.) Consider the following passages from Lifton's 1961 book *Thought Reform and the Psychology of Totalism: A Study of "Brainwashing" in China.*

> [Quoting a released prisoner, Dr. Charles Vincent] "In the cell, you work in order to recognize your crimes. ... They make you understand your crimes are very heavy. You did harm to the Chinese people. You are really a spy, and all the punishment you received was your own fault. ... In the cell, twelve hours a day, you talk and talk—you have to take part—you must discuss yourself, criticize, inspect yourself, denounce your thought. Little by little you start to admit something, and look to yourself only using the 'people's judgment.'" (p. 27)
>
> For eight days and nights, Vincent experienced this program of alternating struggle and interrogation, and was permitted no sleep at all. Moreover, he was constantly told by his cellmates that he was completely responsible for his own plight. ("You want the chains! You want to be shot! ... Otherwise, you would be more 'sincere' and the chains would not be necessary.") He found himself in a Kafka-like maze of vague and yet damning accusations: he could neither understand exactly what he was guilty of ("recognize his crimes") nor could he in any way establish his innocence. Overwhelmed by fatigue, confusion, and helplessness, he ceased all resistance. (p. 23)
>
> [Quoting Dr. Vincent] "You have the feeling that you look to yourself on the people's side, and that you are a criminal. Not all of the time—but moments—you think they are right. 'I did this, I am a criminal.' If you doubt, you keep it to yourself. Because if you admit the doubt, you will be 'struggled' and lose the progress you have made. ... In this way they build up a spy mentality. ... You feel guilty, because all of the time you have to look at yourself from the people's standpoint, and the more deeply you go into the people's standpoint, the more you recognize your crimes." (p. 30)

While the process in a Chinese political prison is obviously extreme compared with what happens in schools (or corporate "Diversity, Equity, and Inclusion" or "unconscious bias" training sessions), the essence of thought reform matches the conscientization process Freire calls true education. The goal is to get you to recognize your context—after extracting it from you through interrogation and interview—and then to reinterpret it through the proper ("people's" or "oppressed") standpoint until you accept it. This is literally why Freire called his magnum opus *Pedagogy of the Oppressed!* That's the goal of his program: to get people to see their world from the oppressed standpoint. Through endless dialogue with a "facilitator," and indeed in peer-learning groups (another hallmark of Freirean "education" that has been grafted onto the "scaffolding" programs derived from Lev Vygotsky), you are urged more and more into seeing your circumstances through the Marxist lens that interprets "oppression" until you are reborn into solidarity with the oppressed.

It's no coincidence, then, that Lifton, like Freire on conscientization, also explains that the primary purpose of the thought-reform (*brainwashing*) process in Chinese Communist prisons is to effect a psychic *death and rebirth.*

> Both Dr. Vincent and Father Luca took part in an agonizing drama of death and rebirth. In each case, it was made clear that the "reactionary spy" who entered the prison must perish, and that in his place must arise a "new man" resurrected in the Communist mold. Indeed, Dr. Vincent still used the phrase, "To die and be reborn"— words which he had heard more than once during his imprisonment.
>
> Neither of these men had himself initiated the drama; indeed, at first both had resisted it, and tried to remain quite outside of it. But their environment did not permit any sidestepping: they were forced to participate, drawn into the forces around them until they themselves began to feel the need to confess and to reform. *This*

penetration by the psychological forces of the environment into the inner emotions of the individual person is perhaps the outstanding psychiatric fact of thought reform. The milieu brings to bear upon the prisoner a series of overwhelming pressures, at the same time allowing only a very limited set of alternatives for adapting to them. In the interplay between person and environment, a sequence of steps or operations—of combinations of manipulation and response—takes place. All of these steps revolve about two policies and two demands: the fluctuation between assault and leniency, and the requirements of confession and reeducation. The physical and emotional assaults bring about the symbolic death; leniency and the developing confession are the bridge between death and rebirth; the re-education process, along with the final confession, create the rebirth experience.

Death and rebirth, even when symbolic, affect one's entire being, but especially that part related to loyalties and beliefs, to the sense of being a specific person and at the same time being related to and part of groups of other people—or in other words, to one's sense of inner identity. (*Thought Reform and the Psychology of Totalism*, p. 66)

For Freire, you are reborn into *conscientization*, and your identity emerges in solidarity with the oppressed as a conscious, knowing Subject and maker of History. It's the same process in two different settings.

Although the educator in the domesticating model always remains the educator of learners, the educator for freedom has to die, so to speak, as the exclusive educator of learners, that is, as the one educating them. Conversely, the educator must propose to learners that they too die as the exclusive learners of educators so that they can be reborn as real learners—educators of the self-educator and self-learner.

Without this mutual death and rebirth, education for freedom is impossible. (*The Politics of Education*, p. 105)

To repeat the crucial construction for this Freire gives later in *The Politics of Education,*

> This Easter, which results in the changing of consciousness, must be existentially experienced. The real Easter is not commemorative rhetoric. It is praxis; it is historical involvement. The old Easter of rhetoric is dead—with no hope of resurrection. It is only in the authenticity of historical praxis that Easter becomes the death that makes life possible. But the bourgeois world view, basically necrophiliac (death-loving) and therefore static, is unable to accept this supremely biophiliac (life-loving) experience of Easter. The bourgeois mentality—which is far more than just a convenient abstraction—kills the profound historical dynamism of Easter and turns it into no more than a date on the calendar.
>
> The lust to possess, a sign of the necrophiliac world view, rejects the deeper meaning of resurrection. Why should I be interested in rebirth if I hold in my hands, as objects to be possessed, the torn body and soul of the oppressed? I can only experience rebirth at the side of the oppressed by being born again, with them, in the process of liberation. I cannot turn such a rebirth into a means of *owning* the world, since it is essentially a means of *transforming* the world. (*The Politics of Education,* p. 123)

Lest the point be missed, let me point out that Freire also makes it, less gratuitously, in *Pedagogy of the Oppressed* as well:

> Conversion to the people requires a profound rebirth. Those who undergo it must take on a new form of existence; they can no longer remain as they were. Only through comradeship with the oppressed can the converts understand their characteristic ways of living and behaving, which in diverse moments reflect the structure of domination. (*Pedagogy of the Oppressed,* p. 61)

Of note, the thought-reform prisons employed by Mao Zedong in China were a specialized recreation of the *gulags* used by Lenin and Stalin in the USSR. Gulags are not concentration camps like the Nazis employed on Jews and other enemies. They were *reeducation* prisons that combined rudimentary thought-reform with reform through forced hard labor, all meant to bring you to see the world and yourself from the standpoint of "the people." The hammer and the sickle represent real work, which will remake you once you learn to recognize it! *Arbeit macht frei*—the work will set *us* free. As Lifton notes, particularly intractable cases in Maoist China were moved out of thought-reform prisons into other more brutal prisons that re-educated by labor (that is, gulags). In this regard, thought-reform prisons are in some sense a more sophisticated tool than the brutal gulags of Stalin, and Freirean education represents a further sophistication of the method that insinuates it, as Mao also did, throughout all of society.

The Stages of Conscientization

Conscientization, again, is the chief *goal* of the Freirean educational program. It's a big word that means exactly what it seems to imply: the process of awakening critical consciousness, which is neo-Marxist activist consciousness. It is becoming "conscious" to one's political context as a Critical Marxist (or, today, a Woke Marxist); it is learning to "recognize" the conditions of your life from the oppressed standpoint as well as your role in perpetuating them and potential for overthrowing them.

Marxist thinkers, neo- or otherwise, especially since the 1920s have been primarily concerned with the process of becoming conscious to the "realities" of society and the "need" to create systemic change. Marx, they realized, had been wrong. Consciousness won't spontaneously arise (from the preaching of the Communist gospel and intolerable working conditions). Worse, when push comes to shove, say in the eruption of a World War, workers of the world stop uniting and hole up in their national identities. Consciousness has to be raised, deliberately and carefully.

This gave rise to a whole new chapter in Marxist thought: Cultural Marxism, which sought to address these issues. Perhaps most notably among Marxist Theorists in this regard is the Hungarian Marxist György Lukács, who developed the concept considerably in his 1923 book (arguably his *magnum opus*), *History and Class Consciousness*. Paulo Freire seems to lean very heavily on Lukács's formulation of consciousness and its development—as the formulations are very similar—and his ideas about conscientization (*conscientização* in Freire's Portuguese) mirror those of his Hungarian predecessor. In particular, Lukács maintained that consciousness was *educable* and *graduated*, that is, it can be taught and arrives in stages. For what it is worth, Lukács served as the Deputy Commissar of Education in the short-lived Hungarian Soviet Republic under Béla Kun in 1919.

For both Lukács and Freire, critical consciousness is not merely something that you have or don't (*nota bene*: Lukács does not refer to it as *critical* consciousness way back in 1923 but retains the earlier Marxian term "*class* consciousness"). There are levels to a Marxist political consciousness, and these levels are awakened to progressively in stages.

It would be foolish to believe that this criticism and the recognition that a post-utopian attitude to history has become *objectively possible* means that utopianism can be dismissed as a factor in the proletariat's struggle for freedom. This is true only for those stages of class consciousness that have really achieved the unity of theory and practice described by Marx, the real and practical intervention of class consciousness in the course of history and hence the practical understanding of reification. And this did not all happen at a single stroke and in a coherent manner. For there are not merely national and "social" stages involved but there are also gradations within the class consciousness of workers in the same strata. (*History and Class Consciousness*, p. 78)

For Freire, this is the point of a "political" education, then: developing through the stages of conscientization. This view elaborates on Marx's earlier concepts about class consciousness. In all cases, the structural underclass has to realize it is a marginalized underclass, then it has to realize the structure is what marginalizes it, then it has to comprehend that the structural overclass gets to determine the parameters of the structure and thus dominates and oppresses them, but this is only the first part of conscientization. Following Marx, the awakening underclass (the conscious "proletariat") must understand that it is a "conscious subject" within the structural reality in which it is oppressed, and, further, as such it has a unique role to play in changing the course of History toward greater liberation. Proletarians must realize that they are change agents who understand the proper development of the world, humanity, and human societies.

In some sense, Marx missed this crucial fact of conscientization. For him, there seem to be four stages of awareness: class-unconscious, crude communism, class-conscious proletariat, and true (transcendent) Communism. That is, there are people who don't understand what's going on, people who have come to hate capitalism and private property, people who have awakened to their ability to transform History as such, and people who have transcended private property altogether as fully awakened men. Marx devoted some ink to the problem of getting stuck in crude communism but didn't flesh these ideas out in nearly the depth we see from Lukács, which Freire developed further into a program that requires virtually nothing of its activists except a Critical disposition (gnosiological attitude).

In short, we could summarize the stages of conscientization this way, as a series of beliefs one has to be reformed or groomed into believing (though these are my labels and descriptions, not how Lukács or Freire describes them):

1. Class Awareness—Awareness that you are a member of a class in a class society.

2. The Nature of Class Society—Class society dehumanizes those whom it oppresses.

3. Holistic Understanding—All classes are part of a broader whole of society, which implies that "oppression" is a verb occurring within a structural dynamic between oppressors and those whom they oppress, all of whom are dehumanized by the process: there is no marginalized without marginalization and no marginalization without a marginalizer.

4. Conscious Subject in History—You are a potential maker of History who has been prevented from knowing this about yourself through your oppression.

5. Standpoint Knowledge—As one of the oppressed, you possess a special role in the making of History, as the dialectical negation to the conditions of oppression; that is, you have to be a revolutionary who changes History.

6. Class Consciousness (First Real Marxist Consciousness)— You are in class solidarity within your class by virtue of your oppression and have a role to play in ending oppression entirely through revolution. But! Class society itself is the problem, following Marx, a profound contradiction. Up to this point, the progression agrees with Lukács.

7. Critical Consciousness (Second Marxist Consciousness; Critical Marxist Consciousness; Marcusian Consciousness)— Because class society itself is the problem, the basic terms of class society are what need to be overthrown because otherwise the Class Consciousness will reproduce class society all over again (think Lenin or Stalin).

8. Utopian Consciousness (Freirean Consciousness)—After any revolution, critical consciousness must increase, not decrease, and the new society that emerges must immediately be criticized and undergo another revolution so that it cannot establish a class society. No vision for the new society can be given lest it be imposed and become oppressive. Perpetual cultural revolution against all oppression.

9. True Marxist Consciousness—The full transcendence of private property, division of labor, division of identities, and any other device that stratifies society (a.k.a., "Social Justice"); arrives after all oppression has been sufficiently denounced that it can no longer be reproduced and Man realizes his true nature as a perfectly Social(ist) being as the stateless, classless (including cultural and identity classes) society emerges. NB: This state of consciousness only exists when everyone (still alive) has it; until then "real Communism hasn't been tried."

The rub for Marxists over the last century is in how to proceed from class consciousness to true Marxist consciousness, as given by Marx himself. The issue is that a class-conscious class thinks of itself in terms of being a class, especially after banding together to effect a revolution, but to achieve true Marxist consciousness, class itself has to be completely abolished. Marx believed this would work itself out dialectically under Socialism (in the dictatorship of the proletariat), and the State would "wither away" when no longer needed to manage class disputes in a classless society. (Note: This means for Marx, the State is how Man is delivered from the Fall by an entity that makes the way and is then self-sacrificial on behalf of our emancipation.) Lenin insisted that in the moment the State holds absolute power, it would become unnecessary and dissolve. This is all obviously (religious) nonsense. Lukács was therefore keenly aware of the issue but did not have the solution in 1923, when he wrote,

Thus we must never overlook the distance that separates the consciousness of even the most revolutionary worker from the authentic class consciousness of the proletariat. But even this situation can be explained on the basis of the Marxist theory of class struggle and class consciousness. *The proletariat only perfects itself by annihilating and transcending itself, by creating the classless society through the successful conclusion of its own class struggle.* The struggle for this society, in which the dictatorship of the proletariat is merely a phase, is not just a battle waged against an external enemy, the bourgeoisie. It is equally the struggle of the proletariat *against itself*: against the devastating and degrading effects of the capitalist system upon its class consciousness. The proletariat will only have won the real victory when it has overcome these effects within itself. (*History and Class Consciousness*, p. 80)

Freire's development attempts to bridge the gap, first by drawing on the half century of Critical Marxist thought (critical consciousness) and then introducing an intermediate stage of pure destruction and blind hope, what I've termed "utopian consciousness." His solution, which he designed by taking cues from what he imagined was going on under Mao in the Chinese Cultural Revolution (which he praised) and that he romanticized in Che Guevara, isn't much of a solution. It's to re-conscientize over and over again and have permanent, perpetual cultural revolution... until it works.

In Freirean pedagogy, walking people through this process of conscientization at least to critical consciousness, if not utopian consciousness, is what replaces learning—it gives the "political literacy" that replaces literacy (which is, in turn, viewed as a bourgeois and colonialist perversion of education). What this means, though, is ultimately that the education isn't just teaching Marxism but is also engaging in Marxist *thought reform*, which is another way of putting *cult programming* or *grooming*.

The goal of Freirean (that is, ultimately, Woke) Marxism is to create and retain cultists who have been groomed to think like cultists in Freire's Woke Marxist cult. Its "hope" exists in believing that no society actually functions at all until the Utopia finally emerges out of perpetual ashes, but this is possible through relentless criticism of any society that attempts to establish itself. The method is Freire's perversion of education into this type of thought reform, which is described in the subsequent sections. The ability to do this is greatly enhanced by the Freirean Marxification of education itself, and this is much of why Paulo Freire proves such a pivotal figure in the theory and practice of education.

There's a great deal going on here all at once. First, since it's based on a Marxist Theory of Knowing, genuine knowledge isn't worth much in a Freirean world. *Excluded* knowledge is to be privileged because it has been excluded, even if it's wrong, especially if it's useful as an activist wrecking ball to the existing society or even the new one activism produces. Second, unlike other Marxist States, which need engineers, doctors, scientists, lots of bureaucrats, and other professionals to make them work until they achieve success and global dominance, Freire's program has no use for such things. It only needs educators and guerrillas because its objective is not to build or establish a functioning society but instead to free men from any such thing.

Of note, a Marxist Theory of Knowing replicates and scales in a way that no other strain of Marxist thought can. *Any* field or domain of thought, from education to physics, from medicine to rock climbing, from economics to environmental science, from food science to theology, can be immediately flung into a Marxist conflict model by claiming that domain of thought unjustly recognizes certain privileged knowledges, knowers, and ways of knowing while excluding and marginalizing others to its own benefit. This is its great strength. Its great weakness is that it necessarily must admit and has almost no filter against "knowledges," "knowers," and "ways of knowing" that are actually horrible, corrupt, made-up, or even insane. In this sense, a

Marxist Theory of Knowing simultaneously dissolves the logic of civilization (indeed, the *Logos* itself) and its own capacity to do anything. As it turns out, however, *its* risk is also *our* risk.

As a result, nonetheless, it is of absolutely no surprise that a Freirean "education" produces know-nothing activists who are good at nothing except complaining in ways that obviously fail to understand what's going on. (For example, why is there "history" and no "herstory" (or "hxrstory")? is a patently idiotic question with surprising activist utility.) The goal of Freirean pedagogy is to produce conscientization of exactly this type.

Generating Conscientization

Again, the Freirean process isn't complicated. "Learners" are datamined through interviews, dialogue, or surveys to find out what (lived) experiences, social and emotional cues, circumstances, and so on, are most likely to radicalize them, though sometimes this content is assumed by the "educator" as facilitator. Social-Emotional Learning is a program exactly designed around this agenda. These "generative themes" are then fed back to the students in abstract form by teachers who elevate them conceptually "as equals," and education focuses on making sure learners know why they are problematic and representative of life in oppression—that is, their life, either as a source or victim of that oppression, or in some ways both at once. Allegedly, achieving academic mastery follows from this circumstance because the increased relevance of the material to their lives increases interest and engagement. In reality, learners become "emotional wrecks" who are then "facilitated" into becoming critically conscious but genuinely ignorant radicals.

Consider an example. In a 2021 education paper titled "Drag Pedagogy: The Playful Practice of Queer Imagination in Early Childhood," the authors, Harper Keenan (who is trans) and "Lil Miss Hot Mess" (real name Harris Kornstein, who is a drag queen integral to

the Drag Queen Story Hour brand and program), present a "drag pedagogy," which is a theory of education rooted in drag performance. They
describe it explicitly as a *generative* practice that brings up themes of identity to young children in the early childhood education environment.

> In recent years, a programme for young children called Drag Queen
> Story Hour (DQSH) has risen to simultaneous popularity and con-
> troversy. This article, written collaboratively by an education scholar
> and a drag queen involved in organizing DQSH, contextualizes the
> programme within the landscape of gender in education as well as
> within the world of drag, and argues that Drag Queen Story Hour
> provides a generative extension of queer pedagogy into the world of
> early childhood education.[17]

DQSH raises questions and dialogue that are then used to present
lessons from within Queer Marxist Theory under the programmatic
branding of Comprehensive Sexuality Education. Their agenda is
explicitly stated not as to increase empathy for LGBT issues, but to
use a generative (Freirean) pedagogical approach to encourage children to learn to *"live queerly"* (italics theirs), which is defined as a
(Marxist-style) opposition to any and all norms or conceptions of
normalcy, especially with regard to sex, gender, and sexuality. In other
words, drag queens are brought into the classrooms of young children
to generate the themes necessary to lead them into dialogues about
sex, gender, and sexuality *that concientize them* into a Queer Marxist consciousness of these and related issues (including mental and physical
health). The presence of the drag queen *alone* is said to be "generative."

> Within the context of DQSH, the visual style of the queen serves
> as a provocation that invites inquiry into normative fashion and

---

17 https://www.tandfonline.com/doi/full/10.1080/03626784.2020.1864621

embodiment. Glitter, sequins, wigs, and heels all serve as pedagogical tools, inviting questions like why and how is drag made unusual in this environment? In other words, while verbal communication is a crucial element of DQSH, even if the queen said nothing, we argue that her mere aesthetic presence would be generative. While simultaneously destabilizing many of the mundane assumptions of gendered embodiment and of classroom life through the style, movement, and gesture, DQSH presents a queer relationship to educational experience. The traditional role of the teacher, transformed into a loud and sparkling queen, becomes delightfully excessive. She is less interested in focus, discipline, achievement, or objectives than playful self-expression. Her pedagogy is rooted in pleasure and creativity borne, in part, from letting go of control.

Once this model is accepted, through drag queens or otherwise, education has to become a process of awakening people to believing this concept of the existing educational system and forging a "critical" path to a new one that is "liberatory," according to Freire.

> If we don't transcend the idea of education as pure transference of a knowledge that merely describes reality, we will prevent critical consciousness from emerging and thus reinforce political illiteracy.
>
> If our power of choice is really revolutionary, we have to transcend all kinds of education in order to achieve another, one in which to know and to transform reality are reciprocal prerequisites. (*The Politics of Education*, p. 104)

In this passage, we immediately recognize first that it mirrors Karl Marx's insistence (in his *Economic and Philosophic Manuscripts* of 1844) that *true Communism* means the transcendence of private property entirely, not merely its abolition. Freire is offering a pure Marxist Theory of education and knowing. We also see an explicit call to decolonize curricula, which is disconnected and domesticating to Freire. Further, there's an explicit call to push into a wholly new form of education that can cause a critical consciousness to emerge. That other kind of education is conscientization, which is therefore revealed to be *not education* on any existing terms. Again, the process of this new kind of education is therefore *thought reform*, a complete revamping of the thinking process consistent with what conscientization represents.

Practically speaking, the now almost ubiquitous program in education known as Transformative Social-Emotional Learning is the main way by which Freirean conscientization is achieved in our schools. While Social-Emotional Learning hasn't always been the "Transformative" model, which is Freirean and explicitly seeks to conscientize as one of its major programmatic goals, virtually all of SEL today either *is* transformative already or *will trend* in that direction (there will be no safeguarding a different model for long). Transformative SEL is designed around presenting generative themes in education relevant to "social and emotional intelligence" and then using "social and emotional" education to facilitate the right under-standing of those concepts and circumstances in the learners. It begins with a data-mining process to identify which themes will work best with which children (among other wholly inappropriate goals). Under a new program of "Systemic SEL," it is meant to be infused into every subject so that every subject is taught with a grounding in SEL and its aims, thus reproducing the generative themes hijacking of education.

Conscientization Replaces Learning

The goal of conscientization as a new form of education is given explic-itly in Marxist terms: "to know and transform reality." A Freirean approach to education, then, can be expected to fail to teach students anything within the range of goals of actual education. Indeed, it aims to *transcend* that objective (and the "private knowledge" it produces) in the same way Marxist Communism aims to transcend private property. Instead, it will teach them to be discontented Marxists political activists, which is broadly what we observe occurring in our schools today—for example in Providence, Rhode Island, and approximately everywhere else. Freire is abundantly clear about this reorientation of priorities:

> As an event calling forth the critical reflection of both the learners and educators, the literacy process must relate *speaking the word* to *transforming reality*, and to man's role in this transformation. Perceiving the significance of that relationship is indispensable for those learning to read and write if we are really committed to liberation. Such a perception will lead the learners to recognize a much greater right than that of being literate. They will ultimately recognize that, as men, they have the right to have a voice. (*The Politics of Education*, p. 51)

In this short excerpt, we see a lot of what's under the hood in the Freirean "conscientization" as education model. In addition to everything already remarked upon, we see that activism is primary and being literate—as the result of a literacy program—is, at best, secondary. Specifically, we see that a conscientizing political education is considered a fundamental right that exceeds the "right" to be literate or educated at all. As previously mentioned, we also see that conscientization is an unfolding process, not an event, for Freire.

It is not enough for a Freirean "learner" to see himself as caught in oppressive or bad circumstances to be conscientized to the "actualities" of his life. He also has to understand that as an oppressed person, he can become increasingly politically conscious, gain a political voice, and thus be a "change agent" who transforms reality and, as he puts it elsewhere, "mak[es] history that actualizes [his life]" (p. 103). Further, it isn't even enough to realize that he can become politically conscious and vocal and thus potentially make change, he must also understand his own role in the transformation process. That is, he has to become *self-conscious* of himself as a creative subject and political change-agent, which is updated from Marx's basic ontology of Man as conscious creator. Freire even articulates this point by quoting Marx and then elaborating upon his explanation of what makes Man fundamentally different from animals. Indeed, he does so several times and in sufficient depth to span many pages. For example,

> Unlike men, animals are simply in the world, incapable of objectifying either themselves or the world. They live a life without time, properly speaking, submerged in life with no possibility of emerging from it, adjusted and adhering to reality. Men, on the contrary, who can sever this adherence and transcend mere being in the world, add to the life they have the existence which they make. To exist is thus a mode of life that is proper to the being who is capable of transforming, of producing, of deciding, of creating, and of communicating himself.
>
> Whereas the being that merely lives is not capable of reflecting upon itself and knowing itself living in the world, the existent subject reflects upon his life within the very domain of existence, and questions his relationship to the world. His domain of existence is the domain of work, of history, of culture, of values—the domain in which men experience the dialectic between determinism and freedom. (*The Politics of Education*, p. 68)

For Freire, what sets men apart from animals is that they can envision what they want to create in the world, including in terms of themselves and their own society, and then bring it into being. Of course, Freire is just repeating Marx here, namely the creative subject-object relationship that Marx said gives rise to man's "species-being," which is something like his true nature. More than that, though, men can understand themselves as creators as such. Like gods, they can imagine what they would see in the world and then bring it into being, and by seeing it created, they can know themselves to be the being that created it. This notion holds a lot of power for Marx, and is central to the Freirean concept of education, by which man learns to make himself and his society (which, in turn, remakes *him* in the next turn). This represents, in some sense, a key aspect of conscientization, and it is why Freire is so insistent on overthrowing the "banking model" of education for his own. The so-called banking model, he argues makes the learner a mere object of the teacher's knowledge and teaching process (pedagogy) rather than a conscious subject in his own educational process.

Conscientization goes further for Freire, though, largely following Lukács and Marx before him. Man isn't just able to understand himself in terms of his capacity to create, and thus his nature as *not-animal* (there's almost an existential scream in how both Marx and Freire approach that issue). Man is also able to understand that he's creating himself *and the limitations that prevent his liberation*. For Marx, the activity of men in society gives rise to the social relations that, through "material determinism," make him who he is by delimiting the range of his subjectivity, thus creative capacity. Freire adopts the same idea, though the conditions are now both material and cultural/*structural*, and expresses it this way:

> Conscientization is viable only because men's consciousness, although conditioned, can recognize that it is conditioned. This "critical" dimension of consciousness accounts for the goals men assign to their transforming acts upon the world. Because they are able to have goals, men alone are capable of entertaining the result of their action even before initiating the proposed action. They are beings who project. (*The Politics of Education*, pp. 69–70)

We already encountered Freire's purpose with this approach: it's to overcome "domestication" through education and replace it with "humanization." As we saw, this goal is every bit as Marxist as everything else in Freire's thought. At least he's quite explicit about it:

> For men, as beings of praxis, to transform the world is to humanize it, even if making the world human may not yet signify the humanization of men. It may simply mean impregnating the world with man's curious and inventive presence, imprinting it with the trace of his works. The process of transforming the world, which reveals this presence of man, can lead to his humanization as well as his dehumanization, to his growth or diminution. These alternatives reveal to man his problematic nature and pose a problem for him, requiring that he choose one path or the other. Often this very process of transformation ensnares man and his freedom to choose. Nevertheless, because they impregnate the world with their reflective presence, only men can humanize or dehumanize. Humanization is their utopia, which they announce in denouncing dehumanizing processes. (*The Politics of Education*, p. 70)

Not to beat a dead horse here, but the (Critical) Marxist utopianism at the heart of the Freirean project is utterly undeniable as the *centerpiece* of that project. A Freirean education therefore shows itself to be little interested in actual education and very interested in outright crackpottery. As a result, the Freirean schools your kids probably go to is organized to turn your kids into utopian crackpots. Rather than learning basic academic skills or pursuing academic excellence, they're taught instead to "speak the word to proclaim the world" with their "voice" as activists—say, through encounters with grown men who dress and act like highly sexualized, irreverent, provocative women (drag queens). As it turns out, his method is completely destructive and lacking in any substantive capacity to build anything.

Announcing Through Denouncing

This transformative speaking is meant to be accomplished by a utopian-magic process Freire describes as "annunciation and denunciation," which are, because of the crackpot utopian nature of the whole program, literally the same thing. (Maybe your child will learn to denounce the society that says men shouldn't dress and act like highly sexualized, irreverent, provocative women and then apply that act and provocation to young children.) For Freire, learning to speak Critical Theory from a critically conscious position enables you to speak a new world into existence *by denouncing the current, oppressive world* in the right terms (from the people's standpoint, adopting a "gnosiological attitude").

> In this sense the pedagogy that we defend, conceived in a significant area of the Third World, is itself a utopian pedagogy. By this very fact it is full of hope, for to be utopian is not to be merely idealistic or impractical but rather to engage in denunciation and annunciation. Our pedagogy cannot do without a vision of man and of the world. It formulates a scientific humanist conception that finds its expression in a dialogical praxis in which the teachers and learners together, in the act of analyzing a dehumanizing reality, denounce it while announcing its transformation in the name of the liberation of man.
>
> For this very reason, denunciation and annunciation in this utopian pedagogy are not meant to be empty words, but an historic commitment. Denunciation of a dehumanizing situation today increasingly demands precise scientific understanding of that situation. Similarly, the annunciation of its transformation increasingly requires a theory of transforming action. Yet, neither act by itself implies the transformation of the denounced reality or the establishment of that which is announced. Rather, as a moment in a historical process, the announced reality is already present in the act of denunciation and annunciation. (*The Politics of Education*, p. 57)

Showing up on the statehouse steps, illiterate and innumerate, to demand change on gun control in Providence because of a failure of law enforcement in Texas is an example of what Freire is talking about with denouncing a "dehumanizing situation." It's what he means by taking "transforming action." Virtually all of the activism, like associated with Black Lives Matter or the implosion of The Evergreen State College, in the ongoing American Cultural Revolution is a clear example of what Freire is talking about, and realizing our kids go to Paulo Freire's schools makes it perfectly clear why those circumstances unfolded the way they did. Your kids are next unless we stop this.

What a utopian project looks like—or, rather, doesn't—is another central issue of Freire's thoughts on conscientization. The political Right, he repeatedly makes clear, *cannot* be utopian, by definition. Furthermore, if a movement knows what it is announcing, it will find itself on the Right by default.

> Thus, revolutionary leadership falls into internal contradictions that compromise its purpose, when, victim of a fatalist concept of history, it tries to domesticate the people mechanically to a future the leadership knows *a priori*, but thinks the people are incapable of knowing. [Here, Freire is plainly thinking of Stalin.] In this case, revolutionary leadership ceases to be utopian and ends up identified with the right. The right makes no denunciation or proclamation, except, as we have said, to denounce whoever denounces it and to proclaim its own myths.
>
> A true revolutionary project, on the other hand, to which the utopian dimension is natural, is a process in which the people assume the role of subject in the precarious adventure of transforming and recreating the world. (*The Politics of Education*, p. 82)

For Freire, then, a utopian project looks like using Critical Theory to denounce every "problematic" aspect of the existing world, which intrinsically announces new possibilities that might be otherwise, even though no one can say what they are or how they would work, lest they cease being utopian, become "sclerotic" and "bureaucratic," and necessarily find themselves on the anti-utopian Right. Instead, they are to assume the role of a conscious subject "in the precarious adventure of transforming and recreating the world" by the magical tool of "announcing" *by denouncing* on Marxist terms whatever they encounter and don't like. In practical terms, this means a Freirean education will teach "learners" to complain according to the methods of Critical Marxism *and almost nothing more*, except occasionally by accident. It's worth pausing, then, to remember Marx's famous rejoinder that his method involves "ruthless criticism of all that exists," which he seems to have derived from a line from his favorite poet. Goethe, in *Faust*, put into Mephistopheles's evil mouth the idea that all truth is relative because *"all that exists deserves to perish."*[18] Unfortunately, many parents and teachers will recognize exactly these results from the education system we have today, in which your kids go to Paulo Freire's schools.

The Perpetual Revolution

As explained in the previous chapter, the solution Freire offers to this dismal read on life, literally, is to hold up the models of Che Guevara and the Chinese Cultural Revolution—where the brainwashing occurred—as clear success stories that avoid this anti-utopian right-wing trap of having some idea what you're going for beyond perpetual uninformed complaint, chaos, and revolution, led by the "conscious" who were "conscientized" to believe this is the most crucial aspect not just of their educations and lives but of their very being as humans. Again, this has to be understood *literally* as what Freire advocates:

18   The in-house glossary of terms on the website marxists.org applies this quote from Goethe in its definition of "truth" from the Marxist perspective. Goethe may not have subscribed to this view, but quoting Mephistopheles from Goethe's *Faust* was one of Marx's favorite literary activities.

Sometimes perpetuation of the bourgeois ideology is expressed in a strange type of idealism that promises that once the transformation of the bourgeois society is achieved, a "new world" will be automatically created.

In truth, the new world does not surface this way. It comes from that revolutionary process which is permanent and does not diminish when the revolution achieves power. The creation of this new world, which should never be made "sacred," requires the conscious participation of all the people, the transcendence of the dichotomy between manual and intellectual labor, and a form of education that does not reproduce the bourgeoisie.

One of the great merits of the Chinese Cultural Revolution was its rejection of static, antidialectical, or overconservative concepts of China's history. Here there seems to be a permanent mobilization of the people in the sense of consciously creating and re-creating society. In China, to be conscious is not a slogan or a ready-made idea. To be conscious is a radical way of being, a way characteristic of humanity. (*The Politics of Education*, p. 106)

Of course, aside from teaching children to destroy Chinese historical culture and shame and kill their parents, the method of education and re-education established by Mao Zedong to achieve this "success" is precisely the thought-reform (brainwashing) process he employed to reorient people to the "people's standpoint." Freire reoriented it, moved it into schools, and called it a *pedagogy of the oppressed*. Why? And what does this entail? Precisely what I called the need for *utopian consciousness* as a late stage in the conscientization process.

Because men are historical beings [that is, Marxists, once conscious of that fact], incomplete and conscious of being incomplete, revolution is as natural and permanent a human dimension as is education. Only a mechanistic mentality holds that education can cease at a certain point, or that revolution can be halted when it attains power. To be authentic, revolution must be a continuous event. Otherwise it will cease to be revolution, and will become sclerotic bureaucracy. (*The Politics of Education*, p. 89)

As a result of the "need" for revolution to be (or become) *continuous*, the conscientization process must also be continuous. In fact, even if the revolution is achieved, for Freire, this is merely an indication that *more* conscientization is necessary so the revolution can continue and, in fact, become *permanent*. As the new world that is announced is brought into being (by nothing more than denouncing the old one in the Critical Theory way), it is already becoming the new old world that has to be denounced so an ever newer one can be announced (because the denunciation came from a critically conscious place). This means that critical consciousness must *always deepen*. You must "do the work" eternally, as a lifelong commitment to an ongoing process, one might say. In fact, Robin DiAngelo specifically says that, and now we understand why. Freire minces no words on this point.

> In the face of a semi-intransitive or naive transitive state of consciousness among the people, conscientization envisages their attaining critical consciousness, or "the maximum of potential consciousness." This objective cannot terminate when the annunciation becomes concrete. On the contrary, when the annunciation becomes concrete reality, the need becomes even greater for critical consciousness among the people, both horizontally and vertically. Thus, cultural action for freedom, which characterized the movement that struggled for the realization of what was announced, must then transform itself into permanent cultural revolution. (*The Politics of Education*, p. 86)

In practice, this isn't merely the pretext for creating some Freirean or DiAngeloan cult. It is also why no matter how much success the always-complaining Dialectical Left achieves, it immediately has to complain more, not just about other things but also about exactly the same thing it just achieved. For one prime example, Queer Theory (Queer Marxism) is Freirean in exactly this sense. It explicitly challenges "heteronormativity," but as it makes progress against this persistent bugbear, it identifies "homonormativity" as a new problematic that needs to be problematized and denounced. What is homonormativity? It's anything that might make homosexuality seem more normal and acceptable, like marriage equality, stable and monogamous homosexual relationships, gay acceptance, and the capacity for gay people to go about their lives without a queer political identity being the most important and front-and-center thing about them. Why? Because as Queer Theorist David Halperin stated in his attempt to define Queer Theory: *queer* is that which *resists* all norms and definitions. And so, they say, the dialectic progresses—through endlessly deepening conscientization.

Sleepwalking Toward Dystopia

In a Freirean education, then, learners are taught to believe that nothing is ever good enough. No matter how much activism they have done or whatever they may have achieved with it, good or bad, there are further problems to be uncovered and denounced, and nothing can possibly be left well-enough alone. Freirean conscientization is therefore a process of being insatiable in one's thirst to complain about things and make them change *somehow* accordingly—specifically without any clear idea what they should change into. In no sense whatsoever can this be called a method of *education*. In fact, it probably barely qualifies as being *thought reform*. It's much more accurately seen as a form of pervasive psychological destruction. Even so, thanks to Paulo Freire's cult guidance, it is exactly the kind of psychological destruction its victims are led to feel good and proud about.

Conscientization always involves a constant clarification of what remains hidden within us while we move about in the world, though we are not necessarily regarding the world as the object of our critical reflection.

I know very well that implied in this critical reflection about the real world as something made and an unveiling of yet another reality, conscientization cannot ignore the transforming action that produces this unveiling and concrete realization. Again, I know very well that to simply substitute an ingenuous perception of reality for a critical one, it's sufficient for the oppressed to liberate themselves. To do so, they need to organize in a revolutionary manner and to transform the real world in a revolutionary manner. This sense of organization requires a conscious action, making clear what's unclear in the profound vision of consciousness. It is precisely this creation of a new reality, prefigured in the revolutionary criticism of the old one, that cannot exhaust the conscientization process, a process as permanent as any real revolution.

As transforming beings, people may stay "glued" to the new reality that comes about from their action, but they will be submerged in a new "unclear" vision.

Conscientization, which occurs as a process at any given moment, should continue whenever and wherever the transformed reality assumes a new face. (*The Politics of Education*, p. 107)

As you can see, for Freire, conscientization put in the place of education is *absolutely necessary*. Why is it so important? Conscientization is necessary because History will not make itself, for Freire, again following Marx. Left to its own devices, History and the men who make it will merely reproduce existing forms. This is the so-called "problem of reproduction" Freirean pedagogy was elevated to solve. "[T]here is no genuine hope in those who intend to make the future repeat their present, or in those who see the future as something predetermined" (p. 58), Freire tells us.

> That is why the utopian character of our educational theory and practice is as permanent as education itself, which for us is cultural action. Its thrust toward denunciation and annunciation cannot be exhausted when the reality denounced today cedes its place tomorrow to the reality previously announced in the denunciation. When education is no longer utopian, that is, when it no longer embodies the dramatic unity of denunciation and annunciation, it is either because the future has no more meaning for men, or because men are afraid to risk living the future as creative overcoming of the present, which has become old.
>
> The more likely explanation is generally the latter. That is why some people today study all the possibilities the future contains, in order to "domesticate" it and keep it in line with the present, which is what they intend to maintain. (*The Politics of Education*, p. 58)

A standard education, says Freire, is geared to produce exactly this outcome—the reproduction of the oppressive present. Therefore, History, thus education, must be consciously made by the conscious (that is, conscientized Woke Marxists). Consequently, Freirean education is a process in which the "educator," as facilitator, guides the "learner" through the process of conscientization so that he will become a "change agent" who understands himself as a maker of History, including his own Marxist liberation. Freire explains that this is achieved through conscientization that, again echoing Marx, allows mankind itself to "emerge from their submersion" and become change-agents, as gods.

> Reflection upon situationality is reflection about the very condition of existence: critical thinking by means of which people discover

each other to be "in a situation." Only as this situation ceases to present itself as a dense, enveloping reality or a tormenting blind alley, and they can come to perceive it as an objective-problematic situation—only then can commitment exist. Humankind *emerge* from their *submersion* and acquire the ability to *intervene* in reality as it is unveiled. *Intervention* in reality—historical awareness itself—thus represents a step forward from emergence, and results from the *conscientização* of the situation. *Conscientização* is the deepening of the attitude of awareness characteristic of all emergence. (*Pedagogy of the Oppressed*, p. 109)

It is in this sense—with reasserted emphasis on the part about man being as gods, though in a far more significant sense even than expressed by Marx—that Freire declares that educators must "live the profound meaning of Easter" (*The Politics of Education*, p. 105).

This is a profoundly religiously flavored expression, in the man-centered theology of Marxism, of a dialectical mish-mash organized to give rise to Freire's famous "dialogical model," which is essentially a process of data mining and cult grooming. Freire explains this in *Pedagogy of the Oppressed* as a necessity to "problem-posing education," which is a precursor to both his "generative" concepts approach and to the more contemporary "project-based learning" approach that is doing little to succeed with students across North America. Adding very little clarity, here is how he had it in that earlier work,

Indeed, problem-posing education, which breaks with the vertical patterns characteristic of banking education, can fulfill its function as the practice of freedom only if it can overcome the above contradiction. Through dialogue, the teacher-of-the-students and the students-of-the-teacher cease to exist and a new term emerges: teacher-student with students-teachers. The teacher is no longer merely the-one-who-teaches, but one who is himself taught in dialogue with the students, who in turn while being taught also teach. They become jointly responsible for a process in which all grow. In this process, arguments based on "authority" are no longer valid; in order to function, authority must be on the side of freedom, not against it. Here, no one teaches another, nor is anyone self-taught. People teach each other, mediated by the world, by the cognizable objects which in banking education are "owned" by the teacher. (*Pedagogy of the Oppressed*, p. 80)

For Freire, breaking free of the existing society is a process of death to the existing society and all of its modes and rebirth as a facilitator in this new classroom structure, which denies on principle any authority to teach or, in practice, discipline students in what became known as "democratic" classrooms. The educator must die and be reborn as a grooming facilitator, and the student must die and be reborn as an empowered, conscious activist. Once this relationship is established, the process of education can be turned toward the Critical Marxist objective of conscientization. As Freire has it, this is to lead your kids, whether or not they can read or write, to possess the necessary perspective on their "actual" conditions to desire and engage in perpetual cultural revolution. Because of the "generative" approach Freire offers, however, he is able to package up this truly awful project as an alternative to learning exactly those things he cares little or none at all for: reading, writing, and the other basics of educational success.

Before continuing to the nuts and bolts of *how* Freire recommends this process should work, let me pose a crucial question to you. If you knew you were sending your children to an identity-based, Maoist-style, Chinese Communist thought-reform prison camp for thirty-five hours a week every week—one that you pay for—what would you do differently than you are doing now?

VI.

GENERATIVE THEMES AND THE THEFT OF EDUCATION

We now turn to *how* the Freirean approach works, rather than what it is and what its goals are. As we already saw in previous chapters, the Freirean method of education essentially proceeds through what he called a "generative themes" approach. A *generative theme* is something that a Freirean educator identifies as being relevant to the "real context" of the learners' lives. That is, they are themes drawn from the lived experiences of the learners, or strategically introduced to them (especially with children), that have perceived and manipulable social, emotional, and political relevance to their lives. They are offered as being more engaging to the learning process than other themes or contexts, so they are used as a pretext to lead with a political "education" as a means of inspiring interest in actual education. It is largely on the back of this specious claim about improved interest, relevance, and engagement in learning that the Freirean method finds its way into educational spaces. Once the "generative themes" approach is understood and becomes identifiable, the grand Marxist heist of education under a Freirean banner becomes immediately visible.

In truth, "generative themes" are concepts Marxists can use to evoke powerful emotional reactions from their students in order to groom them through a process of thought reform into a Marxist consciousness. Trigger warning! In a real sense, they are *triggering* themes because they are "generative" in the sense of generating emotional reactions that facilitators can use to radicalize (that is, conscientize). The real goal of the Freirean method is "political literacy," which means conscientization. That is achieved by using generative themes to trigger priority for political discussions, allegedly as "mediators" to academic learning, and these discussions are to be facilitated by Marxist thought reformers using "lenses" like equity, inclusion, and sustainability.

In the modern context, this process is conducted through a conduit of emotional manipulation known as "Social-Emotional Learning (SEL)," in which educators as some combination of teacher, unlicensed social worker, unqualified psychologist, and "facilitator" teach their students how to navigate the social realities and emotional responses they have to them after discovering and being carefully fed these generative themes. Those generative themes are discovered in an SEL setting by means of surveying (that is, data mining) students, introducing provocative material and gauging student reactions, and through dialogue on political or sensitive social and emotional subjects under the pretext of understanding the underlying social and emotional context in which the students might encounter impediments to learning, especially with regard to social and emotional subjects (including outright Leftist identity politics).

Identifying Generative Themes

Freirean education in its formal sense operates entirely through presenting generative themes, which means educators have to discover those themes first. According to Freire, these themes are *always* contextual and located in the "actual contexts" of learners lives, so they have to be extracted from learners by one means or another every time the Freirean method is to be used. The method therefore necessarily begins with a phase of "dialogue" or other methods of data mining the learners for the circumstances of their lives. What counts are those themes in their lives that evoke the kinds of discontented and aggrieved emotional responses useful to Marxist conscientization. In short, they're meant to evoke feelings of injustice, unfairness, suffering, and misery, or hope in utopian possibility. Recall, for example, the list of the seventeen generative themes in the disastrous Nigerian Freirean pedagogy experiment: "resources, money, abundance, crude oil, stealing, pocket, begging, plenty, poverty, suffering, frustration, crying, hunger, crisis, dying, death." These were the words intended to be a starting point for their adult literacy program because they're generative of the political context of their lives. Words introduced to American schoolchildren aren't much different. Setting aside directly sexual themes (as with Drag Queen Story Hour), racial issues, and overtly political topics (like parents' political affiliations or income levels), surveys often ask *children* about suicide, depression, anxiety, loneliness, starvation, and death, repeatedly and in particular.

Freire advocates dialogue for this information gathering process, as we'll discuss in a later chapter, but this is partly a product of his times. As just indicated, other means can include surveys—which serve other masters and purposes in addition to Freirean discovery— or merely exposing children to something provocative they wouldn't necessarily otherwise be exposed to, like political topics, sexual content or, quite specifically, drag queens. The Drag Queen Story Hour program, recall, bills itself unambiguously as a *generative* method that induces the dialogue by which the Freirean process (here, with regard to norms, sex, gender, sexuality, and so on) proceeds toward queer conscientization. Already and increasingly in the near future, technology like wearable devices (such as heart-rate monitors), eye-tracking devices, artificial intelligence (including "digital friends"), and more will be employed to generate this "psychodata" about our children to mold their educations but also their economic behaviors and to enable greater sociopolitical control over them. The "generative themes" approach is given as a justification for this intolerable intrusion into our children's minds and emotions—for purposes that are not in any way educational.

For what it's worth, the parallel in the Maoist Chinese thought reform prisons documented by Robert Jay Lifton would be the *interrogation sessions* with judges and other state officials who insinuated various ways in which the (falsely) accused might indeed have been engaged in criminal activity so as to start crafting a (false) confession in which they are conscientized to "recognize their crimes" from the "people's standpoint" in the everyday activities they had engaged in while in China before their arrests. The goal in many of those interrogation sessions was to be generative in the sense of finding circumstantial evidence or psychological weakspots that could be exploited to facilitate the thought-reform and related confession processes.

Hijacking the Curriculum

Curricula can also be generative. In other words, the generative themes can be guessed at in advance and offered as provocations, with the data mining process proceeding along lines defined by student reactions. That is how generative curriculum in a Freirean approach should be viewed: as intentional provocations to test where lines of conscientization can be pursued in the students.

Occasionally, especially with regard to sexuality and gender— or drag queens—books introduced to children in schools today are obviously inappropriate to any reasonable observer. These are clear provocations meant to evoke certain lines of programming. Take, for example, the book *Gender Queer*, which is to be found in countless school libraries in the United States. It depicts adult themes and pornographic cartoons while communicating the idea of young people navigating a confused and fluid sexuality in parallel to navigating the tumults of puberty. This book's generative potential in the domain of Queer Theory is as obvious as bringing "generative" drag queen into the classroom or library to read provocative stories to children.

Often, however, the matter is more ambiguous as to how materials intended to be generative constitute a potential problem, especially where issues of race and Critical Race Theory are concerned. Introducing a book about a figure like Ruby Bridges, events like the Tulsa Massacre, or a development like the Harlem Renaissance, or working through poverty statistics disaggregated by race, do not immediately suggest that something "Race Marxist" is taking place, though frequently teachers, parents, and other interested parties recognize that *something* seems wrong in their presentation. Their intuition isn't lying. The materials are being used *generatively*. Their point isn't what they present but the type of conscientizing dialogue they can be used to facilitate. The materials themselves become, as Freire had it, objects that *mediate* knowing between the educator and learner. Another common example is a poem about a boy's dog that gets run over by a car, a poem that includes a graphic description of the dog's death, which becomes a generative theme for children.

In many cases, especially under the auspices of Social-Emotional Learning, these sorts of generative themes are not just used politically but to evoke *emotional* discussions about the themes. This is consistent with Robert Jay Lifton's italicized remark that the penetration of the brainwashing materials into the emotional lives of the prisoners is the *outstanding fact* of thought reform. Students will be asked how it must have felt to be Ruby Bridges, or a person (who looks) like Ruby Bridges, or a person (who looks) like the racists who owned or sold slaves or someone who discriminated against racial or sexual minorities. A particular angle on this might be to try to get students to explain what it would feel like to be, say, a poor black person who believes the reason they are poor is systemic or structural racism. This forces the children to enter into a state of believing systemic racism is *real* instead of a particular (and purposed) interpretation of the world *through their emotions*, which easily deny logic and evidence.

Of course, the hijacking of actual academic subjects is yet another hallmark of Freirean pedagogy. In particular, it is the component in which education is shifted from "literacy" to "political literacy" and in which "consciousness-raising" (conscientization) elements are introduced *in the guise of* other subjects. A math lesson constructed around race and poverty statistics in that way runs a very high risk of being hijacked into a sociopolitical discussion likely to be facilitated onto Woke Marxist terms, at which point it's no longer a math lesson. Freire's whole approach to "literacy" education is hardly more than this, as both his own writing and evidence about how it creates "destructive fanaticism" indicates. This can make Freirean thought reform exceptionally difficult to identify clearly and thus remove from schools and their curricula. It is often the pedagogical process induced by the materials, not the materials themselves, that is the problem.

In a particularly egregious example of this form of abuse, consider the following passage from an education paper describing using Drag Queen Story Hour as a generative pedagogical practice.

It is undeniable that DQSH participates in many of these tropes of empathy, from the marketing language the programme uses to its selection of books. Much of this is strategically done in order to justify its educational value. However, we suggest that drag supports scholars' critiques of empathy, rather than reifying the concept: drag performers do not necessarily seek identification with an "other," but rather to experience ways of embodying and expressing different aspects of themselves. Rather than walking in someone else's shoes—and trying to understand what it might mean to be a different gender, for example—drag offers a model for participants to try on many costumes and cosmetics to understand how these elements reinforce or alter their own sense of self. In the classroom, this queer dress-up might create more opportunities for young people to experiment with the feeling of how and why seemingly arbitrary changes of clothing and behaviour impact the ways they experience and are interpreted by the world. That is, drag is an imaginative and creative process. It is grounded in building character, both in the sense of constructing a persona and in better understanding one's own relations to others. This approach can support students in finding the unique or queer aspects of themselves—rather than attempting to understand what it's like to be LGBT.

Observe how the introduction of drag as a generative theme for "living queerly" is knowingly sold as an attempt to increase empathy for LGBT people and causes while being intended for something completely different: the generative project of leading children to explore their own (political) queerness or what political queerness means in their lives (and, apparently, narcissism). Typically, it is rare to find examples where a blatant confession like this exists, explaining that the given justification for inclusion in the curriculum is little more than a marketing ploy while the (Freirean) generative program is the real intention. Nevertheless, we can rest assured that it is happening with a great deal of curricular choices in virtually every politically relevant domain in every subject in many schools.

For Freire, teaching "disconnected syllables" and "meaningless" sentences, as one encounters in a phonics-based (or the equivalent) literacy education program, or perhaps in an algorithmic arithmetic lesson like doing long division, misses the key opportunity of education. That opportunity, of course, is to misuse schools to awaken a (Marxist) political consciousness and political literacy, that is, conscientization. In a dysfunctional (or pretend) attempt to kill two birds with one stone, Freire recommends repeatedly throughout all of his major works that literacy education should proceed using what he refers to as "generative words," in literacy in specific, and "generative themes," in education in general.

The first practical requirement that a critical view of literacy imposes is that of generative words. These are the words with which illiterate learners gain their first literacy as subjects of the process, expanding their original "restrictive vocabulary universe." These words incorporate a meaningful thematic of the learners' lives. (*The Politics of Education*, p. 12)

The generative themes approach is little more than a way that Freirean Marxist "Critical Pedagogues" have been able to *steal* education right out from under us. Like the bag of sand Indiana Jones uses to attempt to swipe the gold idol at the beginning of *Raiders of the Lost Ark* it is the enabling tool of the theft of education. It also enables the vast majority of their false justifications for including inappropriate curriculum, like Drag Queen Story Hour, and the pretext for much within the torrent of lies deployed claiming subjects like Critical Race Theory aren't being taught in schools. Generative themes enable education to look like education on the surface while being replaced by a program of Marxist conscientization just underneath, thus subjecting our kids to thought reform while the "clever" pedagogues behind the heist laugh at parents who don't know how they're being cheated and abused. While we argue with them about the flashes of glinting light on the surface of the rippling lake, they're programming our kids in the murky depths. Understanding generative themes allows us to get beneath the lies on the surface and expose the theft of education from our children and societies.

Decolonizing the Curriculum

Before proceeding further, let's take an important detour. Pause to recall that Freire's view is that "formal education" or "literacy" is the result of the process of colonization recast in Marxist terms about bourgeois property. The Freirean pedagogical model therefore allows us to make immediate and complete sense of the otherwise preposterous demand to "decolonize the curriculum" that is virtually ubiquitous throughout education today.

Decolonizing the curriculum means replacing articles of "formal education" or "literacy" (bourgeois intellectual property) with that which conscientizes in the Freirean (Woke) sense. The English literature curriculum has to be "decolonized" by removing Shakespeare because extant cultural objects that represent being educated have to be removed and replaced with something else that can be leveraged to raise a critical consciousness. This is to be accomplished through presenting "culturally relevant" materials (i.e., "generative" materials) instead. Those materials are "decolonized" materials. Mathematics therefore has to be replaced with "ethnomathematics" (and even the wildly nonsensical "mathematx") for the same "decolonization" purpose. Literacy is made generative through drag queens and particular curriculum choices. The 1619 Project has to inform "honest history" that forces us to reckon with the founding of the United States on Critical Race–generative terms. And we could go on endlessly into every subject.

Freire, to be sure, is quite literal about this decolonization process, which he says is *necessary* in order to think on new terms:

> That's why I admire Cape Verde's president, Artistides Pereira. He gave a speech in Praia in which he made an extraordinary statement that has a lot to do with our conversation now: "We made our liberation and we drove out the colonizers. Now we need to decolonize our minds." That's it exactly. We need to decolonize the mind because if we do not, our thinking will be in conflict with the new context evolving from the struggle for freedom. (*The Politics of Education*, p. 187)

Marxists like Freire—though in the preceding paragraph he expresses himself more as a postcolonialist, and he was both—see the existing system as "colonizing" with "bourgeois values" everyone who is oppressed by it. The ideology carrying and maintaining those values is created, maintained, and spread as a literal form of propaganda by those who have cultural power, so the dominant culture automatically "colonizes" those it oppresses. Straightness, for example, colonizes the minds of children who are not conscientized to the possibilities (and "necessity") of living queerly, for example. "Assigning sex at birth" isn't usually but can be thought of as colonizing infants with a "cis-normative" view of sex and gender. This social-imposition–based view is Marxism 101, though. Marx believed the privileged bourgeois elite create ideology to propagandize themselves and those they oppress into accepting the current state of affairs in society, and in the language of postcolonialism, this means the bourgeois values expressed and defended ideologically *colonize* the individuals socialized by them, especially those outside of them, to whom they are alien (and thus alienating).

Now we can understand why what Freire created is a *Marxist Theory of Knowledge* (or *of Knowing*), which we usually recognize by the slang term for it: *being "Woke."* A Marxist Theory of Knowing holds that certain people have privileged themselves as knowers so as to exclude and marginalize other potential knowers and their "ways of knowing" and "knowledges" from the mainstream center of society so as to maintain their own advantage. It is from this status as a valid knower that the "terms of the existing society" are produced—and it is precisely those terms that Critical Marxism exists to challenge and, if possible, overthrow. Those excluded by the knowing system need to become conscious to this fact, process, etc., according to the stages of conscientization, and they must then seize the means of production of knowledge and the status of knowing. Decolonizing the curriculum and "decentering" the wrong kinds of ideas and using generative approaches and "centering" so-called "marginalized knowledges" and "ways of knowing" becomes paramount to revolution.

In other words, "decolonizing" the curriculum, an apparently mysterious educational fad that's done incredible damage in just a few years' time, means replacing existing curriculum, especially when it reinforces the (Western) culture at hand, with potentially generative materials that challenge the existing culture and its terms. Not only is it an attempt at cultural destruction (what the Cultural Marxists called *"aufheben der Kultur,"* abolish the culture), it is also a means to introduce the maximum amount of Freirean generative material possible for the purpose of repurposing the curriculum for engaging in cultural thought reform.

Using Generative Themes

For Freire, a "generative word" is a three-syllable word (for reasons to do with the structure of Portuguese) that also has some political relevance to the learner. For examples, Freire suggests using the Portuguese words for "slum" and "struggle" explicitly as generative words from which to begin to teach literacy to peasants. In the modern parlance, we might call these terms "culturally relevant." Not to belabor it by quoting it yet again, but recall the description of the "generative themes" phase of Freirean education as it played out in the Nigerian experimental context. Notice especially the types of words considered "generative" (and remember, the point of choosing these words, say instead of simpler, one-syllable words, is to teach illiterate Nigerians to read), and observe the effects of applying them in a generative fashion.

Stage Two: The Selection of Words from The Discovered Vocabulary

From the discussions of the learners, the Generative Words written by the team of facilitators were: resources, money, abundance, crude oil, stealing, pocket, begging, plenty, poverty, suffering, frustration, crying, hunger, crisis, dying, death.

These words were later depicted in pictorial form showing the concrete realities and situations in the lives of the people. The pictorial display provoked an emotional state of pity and anger among the discussants, some of them could not talk, while most of them were moved to tears asking the question: Why! Why! Why! Why!

Notice the themes are largely relevant to the Nigerians' lives in the sense that they expose suffering, misery, or a perception of injustice. When those concepts are then codified and fed back into the "generative" educational milieu, they do not induce education but calamity. Those emotional reactions are very useful for inducing people to cult adherence and to take urgent action, but they prove predictably terrible for fostering interest in education.

In general, the generative themes approach to education claims to offer an unbeatable means for teaching academic material, like reading, writing, math, history, science, and social studies. It allegedly "works" (though the evidence plainly shows it doesn't) by attempting to teach every lesson possible by presenting it through some politically relevant, usually negative and oppression-centric, concept framed in the terms of the given subject. Allegedly, this makes the subject matter more engaging because it piques the students' interests and gets them emotionally invested in the learning process, which relates to their lives and the capacity to change them for the better. That's the sales pitch, anyway.

In reading and vocabulary, generative curricula might take the form of choosing the relevant books to raise a particular agenda or presenting vocabulary words that have particular resonance: poor, poverty, misery, starvation, privilege, wealth, oppression, injustice, harm, and so on, with higher than statistical frequency. Or, it might feature certain reading materials with political overtones. In mathematics classes, it might take the form of using statistics lessons or word problems to present particular politically relevant circumstances in the form of math problems. In history classes, it could take the form of tailoring the curriculum to focus on certain types of materials to the exclusion of others, such as slavery or the various civil-rights movements (racial, sexual, and so on)—and so the 1619 Project's purpose, aside from the outright revisionism, becomes clear. In literally any class, but notably within a Comprehensive Sexuality Education (CSE) paradigm, a politically queer teacher might introduce ideas about sex, gender, and sexuality, including through discussing their own lives, by incorporating Drag Queen Story Hour, or merely asking children to draw pictures of their own families, as a means of generating a pretext to discuss sex, gender, and sexuality on the disruptive terms given by Queer Theory. (In a Communist Chinese thought-reform prison, it might take the form of suggesting certain relationships or activities in the prisoners' lives were suggestive of espionage, injuring the Chinese people, or other political crimes.)

The generative themes approach is being utilized any time the general curriculum is being skewed to present a "hidden" (usually very thinly veiled) political lesson as either the secondary or *de facto* primary purpose of the lesson, especially when it's sold as being done to increase learners' engagement, investment, and interest. As the name suggests, the purpose of a "generative" approach is to generate political thought and discussion, which the educator-as-facilitator will direct into a process of conscientization.

Freire's purpose with the generative concepts approach is to hijack academic lessons and turn them into opportunities to have discussions about politically relevant topics on his own Marxist terms. That is, the lesson itself, be that reading, writing, history, mathematics, science, religion, or otherwise, merely becomes a pretext and a vehicle for introducing ideas that will then be discussed in order to facilitate the "conscientization" process and thus the Marxification (psychological damage or destruction, followed by brainwashing) of the student. A real education is a political (Marxist) education, remember, and the purpose of such an education is to conscientize the "learner." This is only possible if class time is largely, if not wholly, devoted to talking about politically relevant topics, and this is most easily achieved by hijacking existing curricula to enable it.

Equity Equalizes Downward

Stepping slightly aside, we uncover tucked in here an important but subtle point about the underlying assumptions of Marxism in full generality and Freirean education in specific. Every Marxist Theory generally assumes that the "privileged" classes will be taken care of by the rigging of the existing system more or less no matter how much you change things. This is because Marxists believe people in the privileged class only succeed by virtue of rigging the system in their own favor and to exclude competitors. (This tells us a lot about how they'll run society if they get control of it.) So, in the paradigm put forth by Critical Race Theory (Race Marxism), for example, whites are assumed to have completely full admissions and job prospects even in an economy that heavily utilizes race-conscious hiring and admissions practices because of their white privilege. Thus, race-conscious hiring, promotion, and admissions ("affirmative action") are not considered discriminatory but reparative. Under certain similar types of feminism (Sex or Gender Marxism), the same is true for men ("what about the men?" is a famous sarcastic reply from feminist women on this point), straight people, and people whose sex and gender identity match ("cisgender"). It is assumed men, especially straight men, will just succeed while women and homosexuals need a leg up, say lots of special scholarship, honorific, and inclusion programs. These adjustments often serve as entry points for radicals to come into and begin to colonize a discipline with Identity Marxist ideologies, policies, and activism.

In education, apart from admissions, this would manifest as an assumption that white students will simply learn to read *regardless of the instruction*, while people who aren't white might or might not without generative "culturally relevant" materials. This view simply assumes that those who would excel academically in the existing system will do so regardless of shifting from an actual educational program into another, be it Freire's "generative" concepts model, Culturally Relevant Teaching, whole-word reading (encouraged in Freirean education), intuitive math or ethnomathematics, or any other similar manipulation. For example, academically gifted students are assumed to be certain to reach high levels of academic success if education caters to the "most vulnerable learners" and if gifted and talented programs—technically a form of special education for intellectually gifted students who have special learning needs as a result of their talents—are eliminated.

In many respects, a Freirean approach to pedagogy proceeds upon the unlikely Marxist assumption that the privileged will always just succeed, no matter what. They are, after all, privileged, which, decoded from the Marxian, means that the system has been rigged by an elaborate, hidden conspiracy theory that ensures their success and essentially everyone else's failure. Therefore, under this assumption, educators don't have to use a rigorous pedagogy. They should use bogus "conscientizing" methods and, in the name of "inclusion" and "equity" should teach to the bottom of the class and using wayward methods. In this way, equity, often forwarded as the goal of a Freirean education model, *equalizes downward* by lowering outcomes for everyone so as to minimize differences. For another example, it is simply assumed students will achieve academic mastery even though their lessons are political, social, and emotional in content.

Indeed, the "privileged" need to be exposed to the nature of their privilege and made to feel *discomfort* with it, literally under a program called "the pedagogy of discomfort." This sadistic "pedagogy" is billed as the only way to force the privileged into a state where they can recognize their privilege and the harm the system they benefit from and thus support causes others (obvious thought-reform program is obvious).

A PEDAGOGY OF DISCOMFORT begins by inviting educators and students to engage in critical inquiry regarding values and cherished beliefs, and to examine constructed self-images in relation to how one has learned to perceive others. Within this culture of inquiry and flexibility, a central focus is to recognize how emotions define how and what one chooses to see, and conversely, not to see. (*Feeling Power*, p. 176)

A PEDAGOGY OF DISCOMFORT calls not only for inquiry but also, at critical junctures, for action—action hopefully catalyzed as a result of learning to bear witness. Just as self-reflection and passive empathy do not assure any change, so the safe project of inquiry represents only the first step of a transformative journey. (p. 179)

In a Freirean system, it is how the generative themes would be introduced to "privileged learners" so as to conscientize them—especially in terms of what they "choose...not to see." As explained in an academic paper on elite private school education to this effect by Susannah Livingston,

When considering critical pedagogical work in the United States, it seems inimical to consider this liberatory work in nonpublic schools, as the majority of students attending these elite institutions are the children of members of and/or benefit from hegemonic and repressive power structures in place. This narrative review chronicles my experiences as a critical educator working in American independent schools. It explores the idea that critical pedagogs in tuition-based schools are uniquely placed to assist the movement of elite students toward places of liberatory and positive praxis by anchoring private school experiences in Freiran pedagogy. It also explores the necessity for the liberatory education of students of privilege, explaining that often after exposure to critical pedagogy, these students both desire and are able to use their considerable resources to humanize and empower themselves, and through this, society—helping to end cycles of oppression.

The way Livingston envisions this occurring is by using the generative approach to get "children of elites" to understand that history is shaped by conscious agents so that they can recognize themselves as such—and become willing to dedicate their "financial and social potential to institute change."

In my experience critically teaching children of elites, there have been a few successful tactics for moving students through phases of Freirian growth and toward necessary decodification of relevant issues. The first is a modification of existing curricula to include a Freirian perspective of the past so that past human decisions and choices are clear and the past can be seen as active rather than passive (Freire, 2000). Teaching the impact of human agency on the past and connecting it clearly to the hegemonic structures in place allowed my students to be aware of the root causes of problems while also empowering them to change the future by showing it is not a set course of events but rather dictated by human choice and response—that it can be influenced by their choices and responses. This is often seen by my private school students as both empowering (because they know they have the financial and social potential to institute change, having become aware of their privilege) and also overwhelming (as they realize the depth and breadth of the work that needs to be accomplished). While I did experience some students framing issues as abstract, and demonstrating a deep unawareness of their root causes, it took me several years to realize that this was often a *first step* toward their consciencization rather than a stopping point when I alerted them to their own oppression.

Not only do Freirean pedagogues look for ways to conscientize "privileged" students to get them to become activists on their behalf (with their, and their parents', considerable resources), this flawed and fundamentally covetous assumption is one key way "equity" equalizes downward. It fails our best on the cruel and paranoid assumption that the whole system is rigged in their favor so significantly that they cannot actually be failed by it (or its destruction).

A Deception Called Engagement

This set of bogus assumptions cuts the other way too. Allegedly, according to Freire, because "learners" are already "knowers" and "concrete persons," the generative concepts are ideally pulled from them in dialogue. In fact, they know things even the educator doesn't, to say nothing of the privileged students. So, an educator of agrarian peasants, like Freire, might ask these peasants to spend time explaining the actual conditions of their lives, in effect data-mining them. From those discussions, politically relevant terms—often like "suffering," "poverty," "exploitation," and "misery"—might be extracted as the sample words used to teach them to read. The goal is to find a starting place from which the conscientization process can begin.

> It is to the reality which mediates men, and to the perception of that reality held by educators and people, that we must go to find the program content of education. The investigation of what I have termed the people's "thematic universe"—the complex of their "generative themes"—inaugurates the dialogue of education as the practice of freedom. The methodology of that investigation must likewise be dialogical, affording the opportunity both to discover generative themes and to stimulate people's awareness in regard to

these themes. Consistent with the liberating purpose of dialogical education, the object of the investigation is not persons (as if they were anatomical fragments), but rather the thought-language with which men and women refer to reality, the levels at which they perceive that reality, and their view of the world, in which their generative themes are found. (*Pedagogy of the Oppressed*, pp. 96–97)

The generative approach is billed not only as better because of its ability to begin conscientization; it is also more interesting and engaging for students, says Freire. Actual education would be alienating because its context is abstract, missing, or imposed from another walk of life (a bourgeois/privileged one), its method is imposition by a teacher, and its content is "meaningless" (in the deeper sense) to the student.

Rather than presenting simple, accessible terms and building up, the generative themes approach uses "engaging" terms drawn from the problematic aspects of the learners' lives and then presents them as the basis for a literacy lesson. It doesn't work. In fact, it's a distracting and disruptive catastrophe, as the Nigerian experiments and Freire's own dismissive kvetching showed. That this method impedes learning the underlying subject matter, either by proving inappropriate to the task, distracting by diverting attention into contentious political topics, or turning students into "emotional wrecks" who don't see the point of learning, is not particularly relevant. Becoming "politically literate" is still considered better than teaching "disconnected" concepts that have no (cultural and Marxist) relevance to learners coded as "oppressed."

Cultural action oriented toward this synthesis begins with thematic investigation or generative themes through which peasants can begin a critical self-reflection and self-appraisal.

In presenting their own objective reality (how and where they are), as in problem solving, during a thematic investigation, peasants

begin to revise their previous views of their real world through codified situations [those in which they face some struggle]. They will
then achieve an understanding of their previous knowledge. In so
doing, they expand the limits of knowledge, appreciating in their
"deep vision" the dimensions that up to then were not understood
and are now perceived by them as "clearly understood."

Again, this type of cultural action can only make sense when
one tries to present it as a theoretical instance of social experience in
which peasants participate. If one is alienated from this experience,
one loses oneself, emptied in a series of nonsense syllables. (*The
Politics of Education*, p. 33)

When this is done through a Critical Race Theory–based (or Ethnic
Studies–based, or multicultural education–based, etc.) perspective, it
might be argued that otherwise students of all ethnic backgrounds are
forced to learn the various subjects from a "white," "Western," and/or
"Eurocentric" perspective, which is disconnected from the realities of
their lives. They might be expected to learn the syntax and grammar
of standard English rather than, say, African-American Vernacular
English (AAVE) or other regional or ethnic dialects or languages.
Mathematics might need to incorporate Indigenous and other per-
spectives as ethnomathematics, for example. Comprehensive Sexuality
Education (and Drag Queen Story Hour) might be brought in on the
pretext of offering "generative" ways to provide educational "representation" for gay and lesbian children—though, as they acknowledged,
that's not actually their real purpose.

For Freire, the rationale for using a generative concepts approach
to pedagogy is straightforward: to get the "learners" to engage with
material that he believes is politically relevant to their own lives (not
mentioned: in a way that Freire himself, as a Marxist, thinks appropriate for his real purpose, which is Marxist conscientization and the
cultural revolutionary overthrow of society). In practice today, this

will mean reframing all content through an "equity" or "sustainability" lens. This will enable the primary educational activity to become discussion about the generative concepts while, as a secondary effect, the putative pedagogical goal (e.g., learning to read in a literacy class) will come along for the ride (except, apparently, in the real world, as evidenced in Nigeria). Setting up a circumstance to place himself into a facilitator's role for these ensuing discussions, as "educator," in order to raise a (Marxist) political consciousness of the context and circumstances of the learners' lives is his explicitly stated goal. His given justification for this bait-and-switch approach to education is that it produces higher engagement by connecting to the learners more effectively at the level of their lived experience while educating the learner in the political meaning and implications of their lives.

Culturally Relevant Repackaging

Virtually the entirety of the program called "Culturally Relevant Teaching" (the other CRT) put forth by Gloria Ladson-Billings (originally in 1995) is a simple repackaging of Freire's generative-themes model that uses racial and other identity politics as the source for generative material (packaged as "cultural" facets of identity groups, branded as "cultural competence"). She did this in two of the three landmark education papers she published in that single year.

> Freire brought forth the notion of "conscientization," which is "a process that invites learners to engage the world and others critically." However, Freire's work in Brazil was not radically different from work that was being done in the southern United States to educate and empower African Americans who were disenfranchised. In the classrooms of culturally relevant teachers, students are expected to "engage the world and others critically." ("But That's Just Good Teaching! The Case for Culturally Relevant Pedagogy," p. 162)

Ladson-Billings, like Freire, appeals to greater student engagement as the justification for these programs, which she explicitly explains in her seminal 1995 papers on the topic exist to fulfill three aims: to create academic success (though she never says how or what this looks like, though she does say it's drawn directly from the Freirean method), to be "culturally competent" (which is to say to know how to employ the generative themes approach), and to awaken critical consciousness—that is, to conscientize. That is, all Ladson-Billings did was repackage Freire into a racial context and pare down on the overt Marxism.

> I have defined culturally relevant teaching as a pedagogy of opposition not unlike critical pedagogy but specifically committed to collective, not merely individual, empowerment. Culturally relevant pedagogy rests on three criteria or propositions: (a) Students must experience academic success; (b) students must develop and/or maintain cultural competence; and (c) students must develop a critical consciousness through which they challenge the status quo of the current social order. ("But That's Just Good Teaching! The Case for Culturally Relevant Pedagogy," p. 160)

"Not only must teachers encourage academic success and cultural competence, they must help students recognize, understand, and critique current social inequities," Ladson-Billings writes in the other seminal paper on the topic from the same year, "Toward a Theory of Culturally Relevant Pedagogy" (p. 476). Her goal is to "develop students who can both understand and critique the existing social order" (p. 474). Cultural competence, which is sometimes referred to as cultural literacy—by which is meant a kind of political literacy that treats identity political categories like race as sites of meaningful politics of identity—is therefore a prerequisite to Culturally Relevant Education. As Ladson-Billings herself states, this pedagogy is a perfect repackaging of Freire's approach, down to and including the idea that academic achievement will magically occur by virtue of being in an educational environment and being "engaged" in it. The relentless calls for "representation" of politically relevant identities, including racial and queer, fall under this "culturally relevant" heading neatly and are blatantly used for a "generative" concepts approach to teaching these issues in the relevant Identity Marxist ways.

Nota bene, Gloria Ladson-Billings published yet another seminal article in that same year, 1995, along with co-author William Tate, IV, titled, "Toward a Critical Race Theory of Education." It positions her and the intended goals of her pedagogical work within Critical Race Theory in addition to being unambiguously rooted in Paulo Freire's Marxified education. This introduces a worthy and important aside into the topic of Critical Race Theory, which Ladson-Billings welded into the Freirean approach to education (Critical Pedagogy) in 1995 under the brand name "Culturally Relevant Teaching."

Critical Race Theory is, itself, a Marxist Theory of race. In fact, it is Race Marxism (or Racial Marxism, if you prefer). In perfect parallel to Karl Marx's model that a form of bourgeois private property called capital divides society into an oppressive "superstructural" upper class and oppressed "infrastructural" lower class, which are intrinsically in class conflict, Critical Race Theory suggests that a form of bourgeois racial/cultural property called "whiteness" divides society into an oppressive "superstructural" upper class and oppressed "infrastructural" lower class, which are intrinsically in racial class conflict. Marx held that those with access to capital created an ideology called "capitalism" that justifies the existing structure of society, which is based in (structural) classism. Critical Race Theory maintains that those with access to whiteness create an ideology called "white supremacy" that justifies the existing structure of society, which is structural or systemic racism. On and on these comparisons can go because in the same way that culturally relevant pedagogy is a repackaging of Freire's generative concepts approach to education into the racial and other identity-political domains, Critical Race Theory is a direct repackaging of Marxism into the racial domain (other identity political "Theories" like Gender Theory and Queer Theory reproduce Marxism in other "cultural" identity domains—normalcy as property, cisheteronormativity as ideology, queer as the oppressed, etc., etc.).

In this regard, Critical Race Theory (CRT) and Culturally Relevant Teaching (the other CRT) go together hand-in-glove in precisely the same way that Freire's Marxified education theory and the (neo)-Marxist Theory it seeks to instill in "learners" do. Culturally Relevant Teaching is Freirean Critical Pedagogy designed to teach Identity Marxist themes. Freirean Critical Pedagogy, as its precursor, is Marxified education meant to teach neo-Marxist themes. Ladson-Billings still actively pushes *both* concepts (both CRTs) into education today, more than a quarter century later. Critical Race Theory informs and is delivered through Culturally Relevant Teaching, and Culturally Relevant Teaching is a simple repackaging of Paulo Freire's failed generative concepts approach to education.

Learning Loss: Hijacked Time Is Stolen Time

One of the most egregious failures of the generative concepts approach to education Freire introduces is that it not only displaces valuable class time to program students in a particular (Marxist) ideology, it does so while embedding itself and hiding within that subject, making it difficult to identify clearly and root out. *Technically*, Paulo Freire was teaching peasants to read with his method (sometimes). *Technically*, culturally relevant teachers today are teaching subjects like reading, writing, mathematics, history, and science, though the examples are chosen to be "culturally relevant" (that is, generative) and the core of the relevant subject-matter lesson is displaced by dialogue about the impacts of the generative concepts and the feelings those concepts induce. The result, in addition to radical conscientization, is *learning loss*, exactly like we see in Providence, Rhode Island, and like can be guaranteed in the experimental Nigerian schools. Every lesson generatively diverted into raising "political literacy" is a lesson worse than wasted because it isn't just a lesson lost but is one actively being replaced with something destructive to the learners, their interest to learn (instead of becoming activists), and society.

These abuses of both class time and trust would happen far less frequently with a non-generative, academically focused approach to teaching subject matter—precisely the one Freire takes pains to say does not and *cannot* exist based on little more than the standard Marxist conspiracy theory about power and how it structures society.

> It would be extremely naive to expect the dominant classes to develop a type of education that would enable subordinate classes to perceive social injustices critically.
>
> This demonstrates that there is no truly neutral education. An ingenuous consciousness, though, might interpret this statement by attributing a lack of neutrality to an educational practice in which educators simply don't respect learners' expressiveness. This is in fact what characterizes the domesticating style of education.
>
> Education of a liberating character is a process by which the educator invites learners to recognize and unveil reality critically. The domestication practice tries to impart a false consciousness to learners, resulting in a facile adaptation to their reality; whereas a liberating practice cannot be reduced to an attempt on the part of the educator to impose freedom on learners. (*The Politics of Education*, p. 102)

This generative concepts approach, including all Culturally Relevant (or Responsive, or competent, or Sustaining) approaches to teaching, therefore shortchanges students of the opportunity to learn the subject matter at hand while grooming them toward a "political literacy" considered relevant to the "educator" utilizing the method. It is a very subtle form of indoctrination and ideological programming (that is, cult thought reform), and in practice it's a total disaster. Most challengingly for those who oppose it, the political lesson is disguised as a basic-skills lesson in reading, vocabulary, mathematics, or other subjects through the alchemy of "cultural relevance" or "generative words" as an approach.

Here's a very subtle example, courtesy of former educator Jennifer McWilliams, that's unfortunately typical in Social-Emotional Learning approaches to leveraging "engagement." Consider this second-grade arithmetic word problem: "Johnny is riding in the car on the way to the amusement park with his mom and dad. The amusement park is 50 miles away. They have already driven 30 miles. How much further do they have to go?" It seems completely innocuous, but an activist "educator" trained in SEL could easily facilitate this word problem into classroom discussions of poverty, race, sexuality, gender, environmentalism, and parental authority. For instance, she might ask the students who has been to an amusement park and who hasn't to build "engagement." Then before doing the math problem ask why some people have been and haven't been to an amusement park until someone brings up that not everyone can afford it. The teacher used "amusement park" as a generative theme for a discussion about poverty that could easily spin into a discussion about race. "Mom and dad" could "generate" discussions about feminism, sexuality, and gender. "Car" could "generate" discussions about environmentalism. The circumstances of some children having gone and others parents telling their kids they're not old enough yet could "generate" discussions about parental authority and its legitimacy. All of these topics will then be addressed from lenses like "equity" and "sustainability." This is how the "generative themes" approach can easily hijack any academic lesson at all and turn it into an opportunity to conscientize into a desired "political literacy."

The challenge before us is to learn to recognize and call out the *generative themes* approach rather than focusing on specific curriculum items or practices in schools. While the materials can be quite egregious—up to and including adult men dressed as sexualized women (drag queens) presenting sexual material to children and the presence of outright pornography like the book *Gender Queer* in school libraries—the materials are merely "mediating" accessories to the method, which needs to be rooted out entirely.

VII.

CODIFICATION AND DECODIFICATION
AS A THOUGHT-REFORM METHOD

Paulo Freire advances the operational core of his educational program in three steps that many educators and parents today will find familiar from their kids' classroom materials, though not by his name for it: the codification and decodification method. For Freire, after mining learners and presenting ideas through the generative themes approach, the educator, as facilitator, will groom the learner into a Marxist understanding of the theme. The process proceeds by "codifying" a generative theme, concept, word, etc., according to these special rules and "reading" it, then "problematizing" it, and then "decodifying" it. (These correspond to the three-step dialectical approach underlying all of Marxism, wherein some phenomenon is rendered *abstract*, then *critiqued* through a *negative* critique, and then made *concrete* by attaching it to the lived "reality" of the situation.)

Thus, the very first step of the Freirean method then is using dialogue, surveys, etc., to obtain generative content. This content is then used in the operational core of Freirean thought reform, which unfolds in calculated steps. The generative themes are fed back to the students in a "codified" (abstracted) form so the students can decode them. This process of decodification takes place in discrete stages: "reading" the political "realities" contained in the codification, problematizing them, and then connecting them to the "lived experience" of the learners. Freire insists that decodification then continues into the actual literacy lesson, though the evidence doesn't seem to be on his side in making this assertion.

While the issue of *codification* is straightforward and relatively easy to understand, the processes of *decodification* are more complicated. There is a simple reason for this fact. There isn't a single process of decodification occurring; there are *two* at once. In the equivocation between the two forms of decodification, one political and one linguistic—which Freire presents as a single mixed method of creating interest and engagement through political discussion that will be followed by the literacy lesson—Freire hides the primary mechanism for the theft of education. Using generative themes to recenter education around radicalizing (that is, conscientizing) material is the setup. The heist is completed by pretending to do a linguistic decodification that terminates with learning to read but that gets hijacked by doing the radicalizing political decodification *first* and producing the catastrophic result seen in Nigeria.

Overview of the Thought-Reform Process

For Freire, what the codification process amounts to is presenting an image of a generative theme, usually a picture, since he aims to teach illiterates who cannot read. Any material deemed "generative" could be organized into a codified lesson, however. A story about slavery is a codification of slavery, for example, and the presence of a drag queen is a codification of a lesson on transgressing boundaries of sex and gender. The purpose of presenting the image in an abstract form, according to Freire, is so that the learner can gain "critical distance." What this means is that the learner has to be able to comprehend the generative theme through the abstract presentation while remaining detached enough from it to criticize it and what the educator will present as its "real causes." This creation of this presentation out of the generative themes is called "codification."

Then, the oppressive or harmful elements of the image are

discussed. This begins the processes of "decodification." As noted, there are two decodifications occurring at once; one real and political, one fake and the sales pitch. The whole process begins politically with "reading" the situation for its political content, which is then problematized. These are the first two stages of the *political decodification* process, which constitutes the actual mechanism of Freirean thought reform. It turns the codified content *toxic* and makes it *real* and *relevant* to the learner. In other words, this phase is where the Marxist analysis begins. This is where the "equity," "sustainability," or "inclusion" lenses get applied. Its goal is to show the learner why the image and ideas in the codification represent structural injustice and to lay out the "structural causes" of the depicted circumstance, as Marxists perceive them, and why they are oppressive and "concrete" in their own lives.

Finally, the learner is facilitated (groomed) to identify himself with the idea presented abstractly in the image. This is the final stage of political decodification, which results in conscientization and thus seeing the world from the standpoint of the oppressed. Allegedly, the *linguistic* decodification now follows, leading students who are now supposed to be enthusiastic to learn to "decodify" their language and learn to read.

In this way, Freire pretends, not only did the learner learn to read the relevant generative word and become interested in reading more about the issue, but he also learned to read the political context of his life. In reality, actual literacy is sacrificed through a terrible pedagogy for political literacy, which isn't neutral political literacy but the activist agenda of the Marxist facilitator grooming the "learners" to see their world and its problems through a Marxist lens. In the old-school Marxist terminology, this process would be said to "demystify reality." Let's consider this process in three specific examples across two settings: a Chinese Communist thought-reform prison and then two classrooms in a hypothetical elementary-school setting.

In the Maoist prison, various doings of your life are presented to you by the judges in the interrogation process. These are suggestive of crimes you have been arrested for allegedly having committed and to which you must confess. The trouble is, you don't possess the (Communist) "people's standpoint" (*rénmín lìchǎng*, 人民立场) and therefore cannot see how what you did is a crime. The idea of it being a criminal act is abstract to you and presented as *codified*, say as potential espionage, but through interrogation, (Marxist) study (*xuéxí*, 学习), and group "help" sessions referred to in Chinese as "struggle" (*dòuzhēng*, 鬥爭; or *pīpàn dòuzhēng*, 批判鬥爭, "critical struggle"; also called "*denunciation*" sessions), your behavior is made *problematic* against the backdrop of the people's standpoint. Eventually, as you adopt the people's standpoint, the crimes you have been accused of committing become apparent to you; you learn to "recognize" them and see yourself as a criminal against "the people." They have been *decodified*, and your thought has been "reformed."

Next, consider an elementary school covering the idea of slavery in a social studies lesson equipped with Social-Emotional Learning. An age-appropriate book on the topic of slavery might be presented, and so an abstract, codified depiction of the horrific institution is provided to the students through otherwise unobjectionable curriculum items. The teacher, next, as a facilitator, directs the class into a social and emotional lesson on the subject. "How do you think the slaves must have felt?" they might ask, no longer focusing on the facts of slavery but shifting into the emotional components. "How is slavery unjust and unfair?" they might also ask, focusing on white supremacy as the creator of the injustice. "How did people who look like Sally oppress people who look like Michael? What did they get out of it?" they might continue. "How do you think that makes Michael feel?" Social-Emotional Learning techniques then facilitate a class discussion about the topic of slavery where different children are encouraged to speak up about how they might have felt and how it allegedly relates to racism they experience in their present-day lives. Students are facilitated into seeing themselves in the story—into *recognizing themselves and the structural injustices in the given context*—and the causes of the injustice are decodified in terms of the "white supremacy" and "white privilege" that still allegedly pervades and organizes society today. They are accused of racism through complicity in systemic racism and groomed to recognize themselves as racists from the Critical Race standpoint. The process is the same.

Now consider an elementary school hosting a "generative" Drag Queen Story Hour reading session. Children are brought to the school library, where they are presented with a clownish adult man dressed as a sexualized woman who reads to them while performing drag. The concept of gender *and gender fluidity*, and possibly sexuality, is presented to them in a codified form in the person and performance of the drag queen. Questions like, "why are you dressed like a girl?" often follow, according to the purveyors of this "pedagogy," and receive replies like, "why does it matter if people dress as a boy or a girl?" The problematization of gender and sexuality begins with a drag queen acting as a facilitator. Questions like, "who wants to be a drag queen when they grow up?" come from the drag queen himself, easing the children into a decodified "queer" perspective of gender and sexuality. The process is again the same. While only the two in elementary schools explicitly feature the Freirean approach, there is virtually no distinction at the pedagogical level from the thought-reform prison. Why should there be? Both are sophisticated "educational" methods to get people to see their circumstances from the Marxist perspective—people's or oppressed.

Now we'll turn our attention to looking at the codification and decodification process in greater depth.

Codification

Codification—essentially, presenting something "real" and generative as abstract—is the first step after identifying a generative theme.

Technically, codification is something the educator does with the generative themes as a form of lesson planning. It is not something done with the students. The goal of codification is to prepare a Marxist thought-reform lesson based upon the generative theme relevant to the circumstances of the learner's lives while disguising it as an abstract academic lesson. The "codification" process is how the facilitating educator turns a generative theme like "amusement park" into an onramp for a discussion about a Marxist theme like equity.

> It is with the apprehension of the complex of contradictions that the second stage of the investigation begins. Always acting as a team, the investigators will select some of these contradictions to develop the codifications to be used in the thematic investigation. Since the codifications (sketches or photographs) are the *objects* which mediate the decoders in their critical analysis, the preparation of these codifications must be guided by certain principles other than the usual ones for making visual aids. (*Pedagogy of the Oppressed*, p. 114)

The focus here on "contradictions" gives away that it is a Marxist approach. The idea is to present back to the learners the "context" of their lives in a way that generates the feeling that it somehow contradicts with how things "should" be—according to subversive Marxist whispering. You could imagine a Chinese thought reformer suggesting that those seemingly innocent meetings you had with a friend involved passing information to someone who occasionally traveled out of China, so there is a contradiction in your belief that it was merely an innocent meeting. You could similarly imagine a lesson on slavery and white supremacy discussing how the Declaration of Independence teaches all men are created equal but that wasn't the case in America—and never has been and still isn't. You could also imagine a young child's confusion at the blatant contradictions of a grown man dressed and performing as a highly sexualized woman *and* that this clownish person appears and gives a lesson in the otherwise formal school at all (teaching rule-breaking is explicitly stated as a generative aim for Drag Queen Story Hour, according to its mission). The drag queen, we might suppose, "prepar[es] the codifications...by certain principles other than the usual ones for making visual aids."

Now, I want to draw your attention to a key idea in Freire that we discussed in the very beginning of this guide: "the codifications are the *objects* which mediate the decoders in their critical analysis." Freire makes this point repeatedly throughout his books. Here's another example.

> The "codification" that peasants have in front of them is not a mere visual aid, one that the educator uses to "conduct" a better class. The codification, to the contrary, is an object of knowledge that, in mediating between the educator and students, allows its own unveiling to take place.
>
> By representing an aspect of the peasants' concrete reality, the codification contains the generative word that refers to the codification or to some of its elements. (*The Politics of Education*, p. 24)

For Freire, then, the academic material presented as a lesson isn't important for what it is but for what it represents: an opportunity to conscientize. The codified lesson materials are merely a *mediator* the educator-as-facilitator and learner engage in together to reach conscientization. In practical terms, this means that the subject matter—reading, writing, math, history, etc.—isn't all that important in a Freirean educational arena. The academic content is a mere mediator toward conscientization, and the specific material is chosen "generatively" to facilitate (social and emotional, and/or political) conscientization. He repeats this point throughout his books.

> Codification, on the one hand, mediates between the concrete and theoretical contexts (of reality). On the other hand, as knowable

object, it mediates between the knowing subjects, educators and learners, who seek in dialogue to unveil the action-object wholes. (*The Politics of Education*, p. 51)

Codification itself, then, enables the educator to connect what's happening in reality around the learners to the "theoretical context," which is its Marxist interpretation. It then allows the educator to present this poisoned fruit to the learners "as a knowable object" that mediates the conscientization process. Academic content in a Freirean school is a prop, and that prop has a very specific purpose. It is to reinterpret triggering aspects of "lived reality" through some Marxist lens and then to thought-reform "learners" into accepting it as the right interpretation of their "lived experience" and thus the more profound nature of reality itself. Of course, anyone familiar with Transformative Social-Emotional Learning just realized what that entire program is; it's *this*.

Freire's rules for the codification process are interesting in their own right. In fact, there's the usual Marxist tendency toward a peculiar self-awareness-by-projection readily discernible in his description.

> The first requirement is that these codifications must necessarily represent situations familiar to the individuals whose thematics are being examined, so that they can easily recognize the situations (and thus their own relation to them). . . . An equally fundamental requirement for the preparation of the codifications is that their thematic nucleus be neither overly explicit nor overly enigmatic. The former may degenerate into mere propaganda, with no real decoding to be done beyond stating the obviously predetermined content. The latter runs the risk of appearing to be a puzzle or a guessing game. Since they represent existential situations, the codifications should be simple in their complexity and offer various decoding possibilities in order to avoid the brain-washing tendencies of propaganda.

Codifications are not slogans; they are cognizable objects, challenges towards which the critical reflection of the decoders should be directed. (*Pedagogy of the Oppressed*, pp. 114–115)

Somewhat more simply, codifications of generative themes have to meet three criteria to Freire. First, they must be an abstract representation of the theme. Second, they must be based upon emotionally and politically engaging themes in the learner's real lives—that is, they must exhibit potential to *radicalize* the students politically. Third, they have to be organized in a way so that the political content is visible but not obviously propagandizing.

The "generative" potential of drag queens, in specific, is therefore visible. They are "fun," both drag queens themselves and public officials (including Attorney General Dana Nissel of Michigan) tell us. As Freire has it, they're "neither overly explicit nor overly enigmatic." The gender and sexual provocations are obvious but at the same time tucked within a blatant clown. A stripper would be too explicit (while reifying gender instead of calling it into question); a passing and professional gay, lesbian, or trans individual would be overly enigmatic. Drag queens are simple in their complexity and offer various decoding possibilities. That enables the facilitators using them to have plausible deniability about their real purposes—here, about LGBTQ "representation" and "empathy"; in CRT, "we're just teaching honest history," for example. They do not, however, avoid the brainwashing tendencies of propaganda; they *are* that.

For Freire, in the adult literacy context in the colonized Third World, codification proceeds by presenting a drawing of something like a slum or a field being worked by laboring peasants. Alongside the image, the generative concept will later be presented, for instance, the word *favela* (slum, in Portuguese) as caption to the image. This "codifies" the idea of a slum for the learner while preparing him to sight-identify the word "slum" according to what he sees in the abstract image of a slum.

Freire's stated goals through codification are two. First, the learner will be prepared to sight-identify the word "slum" and associate it with the image, after which syllabic (phonics) exercises can proceed. (Imagine a child's first reading word being "suffering," "misery," or "exploitation" for a sense of how ridiculous this is as an approach.) As a result, "conscientization" and "political literacy" are brought into the lesson under the guise of teaching people to read.

Second, the learner will obtain "critical distance" from the contents of the codification. He might live in a slum himself, but he will be able to see it as something *someone else* lives in, or something wholly abstract. This facilitates his ability to *read* it, then *problematize* it, and then reattach to the Marxist interpretation created in that phase through "decodification."

> In our method, the codification initially takes the form of a photograph or sketch that represents a real existent, or an existent constructed by the learners. When this representation is projected as a slide, the learners effect an operation basic to the fact of knowing: they gain distance from the knowable object. This experience of distance is undergone as well by the educators, so that educators and learners together can reflect critically on the knowable object that mediates between them. The aim of decodification is to arrive at the critical level of knowing, beginning with the learner's experience of the situation in the "real context." (*The Politics of Education*, p. 52)

In modern circumstances, generative images, texts, contexts, and other educational contents can be used to portray identity-political (Identity Marxist) concepts to children in schools. For instance, they might read books about slavery and the unjust treatment of slaves and learn to see slavery in the codified context—*not quite* propaganda. This presents a remarkable challenge for people who realize a manipulation is taking place. There's frequently nothing particularly wrong with much of the specific material presented in these sorts of lessons that are ultimately Freirean codifications (sometimes and in some domains, particularly in sex, gender, and sexuality-relevant lessons, it is more obviously egregious or inappropriate—"what does gender mean to you?" or "why shouldn't we break the rules?" asks a drag queen). Codification means nothing more than willfully creating hidden opportunities to turn academic lessons into Marxist political discussions about structural power, which is an intentional theft of education. Because the generative and even codified material is often (though not always) unobjectionable, challenges to the Freirean approach are often rebuffed successfully through gaslighting and public-relations attacks. For instance, challenges to a Freirean codification might be answered with "this is just teaching about slavery," "you just want to ban books about slavery (so you can go back to it)," or "you don't want people to develop empathy for LGBT people," all of which (intentionally) obscure the deeper purpose of the codified lesson and program of thought reform of which it is the second part.

The underlying purpose of presenting codified materials and generative themes, which is *to employ the Freirean process that follows*, is the issue, which can be difficult to draw out. That underlying purpose is to engage in the following steps of problematization and decodification, which groom the learner into viewing the generative concept through a broadly Marxian lens. Codified learning materials may be quite subtle, like having a preponderance of identity-political material as curriculum, presenting circumstances that "raise the issue," or working blatantly political topics into mathematics word problems; or quite egregious, such as employing drag queens, engaging in "affirmation" and "social transition" activities behind parents' backs, or directly bringing up specific topics in an agenda-driven way, which can be particularly outrageous and obvious in gender and Comprehensive

Sexuality Education. For example, this can be done through the book *Gender Queer*, which, for one graphic example, visually and verbally presents the idea of *minor* teenagers exploring the taste of their—and I quote—"vagina slime" and performing oral sex on strapped-on sex toys.

To be clear, virtually all of "cultural competence," Culturally Relevant Teaching, and Culturally Responsive Teaching is a recreation of the codification aspect of Freirean pedagogy into the Identity Marxist "cultural" framing. So is a lot of subtle "groomer" behavior like introducing seemingly "everyday" issues about sex, gender, and sexuality so that the issues of homosexuality, transgender, etc., are raised and then force a discussion. Drag Queen Story Hour proudly sells itself this way.

There are other examples, too. Many states, including California, Oregon, and Washington, wherein these were pioneered, have already explicitly adopted "ethnomathematics" curricula within a broader push for Ethnic Studies. Ethnomathematics bills itself as teaching something like an anthropology or history of mathematics, including various methods of counting, geometry, and arithmetic used by various ethnic cultural groups (especially indigenous) throughout the world. Alternatively, it may teach points like that the number system we use is Arabic and was invented in India, that the Egyptians and Babylonians had the Pythagorean Theorem before the Greeks, or that algebra is a Middle Eastern invention (*al-jabr*, lit. "reunion of broken parts," i.e., the "balancing" of both sides of an equation). The point of all of these lessons is to create generative themes turned into codifications that challenge and complicate a "white, Eurocentric" view of mathematics that needs to be connected to broader narrative arcs, problematized, and used as fodder for radical anti-Western "decolonizing" activism. The frustrating nature of the fact that there's often nothing immediately wrong with such lessons, which can be interesting on the surface, but that they're being used for the Freirean codification-based hijacking of mathematics is the underlying problem.

In my view, this is the real primary purpose of the codification stage of Freirean education: to advance the generative hijacking of other subjects into being vehicles for conscientizing students into "political literacy." Through codification, a political lesson can be disguised as a reading, writing, history, social studies, science, or mathematics lesson. Thus, academic instruction is diverted into political instruction almost invisibly.

Decodification

If the codification is the bag holding the sand Indiana Jones tries to place on the pedestal while stealing the gold idol in *Raiders of the Lost Ark*, decodification is the sand inside of it. (*Nota bene*: The bag is actually filled with shit.) The codification, prepared by the educator from the generative themes, once obtained, is merely the setup to the decodification process. Decodification is the process of conscientization, which is to say thought reform. It is also literally the location of the operative step of the *theft of education* the Freirean method represents.

The entire goal of codification is to facilitate its *decodification* (read: methodological political grooming, or thought reform, into Marxist thought while selling it as a means of increasing engagement so students will want to learn), which proceeds in stages. It's a little confusing to explain the stages of decodification. Freire lists five steps, but in truth there are three. The reason for this discrepancy is that Freire is blending two decodifications together into a single process, one *political* and one *linguistic*. The codification of the generative theme literally is a codified abstract representation of the radicalizing theme that must be politically decoded, but, in another sense, language itself is a codification of the meaning conveyed by the codified image and the circumstances it represents. That is, language needs to be decodified in order to learn to read. This little bit of pedagogical sleight of hand *is the Freirean theft of education.*

To summarize before reading it from Freire, once the codification is presented, the decodification process begins as the "facilitated" educational process. First, the political meaning of decodification is done. This political decodification proceeds in three stages. Then, the students, who allegedly will now want to learn to read, are presented with the word corresponding to the generative theme in the codification. That begins a linguistic decodification: attaching a word to the image and then using that word to teach how to read other words (through syllables, sight reading, phonics, or some other method), using the first word as a starting point to bring up related words.

To see this confusing trick in action, here is a slightly abridged version of Freire's description from a technical appendix to chapter seven of *The Politics of Education*. Note, Freire has already framed out the codification with the example word *favela*, meaning slum.

Stages of Decodification: there are five stages.
   a. The knowing subjects begin the operation of breaking down the codified whole. This enables them to penetrate the whole in terms of the relationships among its parts, which until then the viewers did not perceive.
   b. After a thorough analysis of the existential situation of the slum, the semantic relation between the generative word and what it signifies is established.
   c. After the word has been seen in the situation, another slide is projected in which only the word appears, without the image of the situation: *favela.*
   d. The generative word is immediately separated into its syllables: *fa ve la.* The "family" of the first syllable is shown: *fa, fe, fi, fo, fu*

Confronted with this syllabic family, the students identify only the syllable *fa*, which they know from the generative word. What is the next step for an educator who believes that learning to read and write is an act of knowing (who also knows that this is not, as for Plato, an act of remembering what has been forgotten)? He realizes that he must supply the students with new information, but he also knows that he must present the material to them as a problem. ... [Draw out the syllabic content through questions; repeat with the other syllables, *ve* and *la*.]

    e. Next, the educator asks the learners: Do you think we can (never, do you think *you* can) create something with these pieces?

This is the decisive moment for learning. It is the moment when those learning to read and write discover the syllabic composition of words in their language.

After a silence, sometimes disconcerting to the inexperienced educator, the learners begin, one by one, to discover the words of their language by putting together the syllables in a variety of combinations. (*The Politics of Education*, pp. 92–94)

In this technical vignette, Freire frames decodification as a process of learning to read the word presented with the codified content, discovering the word for what it is (a word), what it's composed of (syllables), and drawing out the idea that these syllables and others can be arranged to create other words, allegedly leading students to discover a way of learning to read the syllables. With it, at least in the early 1960s, Freire reportedly had some success at teaching some peasants to read quite quickly. This is not what Freirean education actually does, though, as we saw in the Nigerian example. This technical description papers over the *political learning* process Freire repeatedly says is actually central to his entire program, the same one that derailed potential learners in Nigeria.

Frankly, all of the political decodification is happening in step (a), as listed by Freire, which seems rather unassuming. The linguistic decodification is then presented in steps (b) through (e), but the trick is that those steps virtually never happen in the Freirean classroom. As the Nigerian experiment shows and the progressive learning loss across America attests, radicalized students aren't interested in learning academically. They want to engage in *praxis*, which is some combination of activism in the world and conscientizing other learners (like the "struggle" groups in Maoist education programs). Thus, education is stolen, and radicalization is achieved with very little academic learning taking place. Of course, a clear symptom of this kind of theft of education would be a shifting of measurement and priority with regard to academic achievement, much like the one we see with Social-Emotional Learning. Academic achievement is watered down by placing it within a far longer list of social and emotional "competencies" the education intends to achieve instead. (They claim "in addition," but this is obviously false both in theory and practice.)

So what's going on in step (a)? The real stages of decodification. These are the three stages of *political decodification*: *reading, problematizing,* and *concretizing* (or, *re-identifying*; or, *personalizing*).

On the front end, the codification itself is meant to give the learner "critical distance"—which is a pun—which enables the first stages of political decodification. The first of these is "reading" (also a pun—learning to "read the room" while pretending to learn to read). The next is *problematization*, in which the injustice within the political reading of the context is revealed. Finally, there is *concretizing*, in which the learner is led to identify himself as a conscious subject and participant in these circumstances and their potential for change. After concretizing, the learner can be said to have been conscientized to the relevant political lesson and to have gained some political literacy.

"Reading" means learning to see the codified situation in terms of structural power, a first stage of conscientization, and problematizing adds the Marxian critique of that alleged power dynamic. It is the opening part of learning to see the world from the "people's standpoint" or from the "side of the oppressed." It's offering a political context to the generative theme. That means it is learning to read the codified context in Marxist terms, which is also to read structural injustice into those contexts.

> The surface structure of codification makes the action-object whole explicit in a purely taxonomic form. The first stage of decodification—or reading—is descriptive. At this stage, the "readers"—or decodifiers—focus on the relationship between the categories constituting the codification. This preliminary focus on the surface structure is followed by "problematizing" the codified situation. This leads the learner to the second and fundamental stage of decodification, the comprehension of the codification's deep structure. By understanding the codification's deep structure the learner can then understand the dialectic that exists between the categories presented in the surface structure, as well as the unity between the surface and deep structures. (*The Politics of Education*, p. 52)

"Reading," here, means reading the politics—through a Marxist lens—of the situation, at which point problematization can begin. In the Chinese thought-reform prisons, "struggle," in which your cellmates "help" you learn to recognize your crimes from the people's standpoint, was accompanied by "study," which means the study of Marxist texts that gave the standpoint its context. In classrooms, it's framing these issues in terms of structural injustices as described by Woke Marxist Theories like Critical Race Theory. The "deep structure" referred to by Freire here is synonymous with the "people's standpoint" or Marxist interpretation. This requires "critical distance" from which the generative theme can be read, which the codification provides. That distance gives the learner room to critique what he sees—at a political level, while learning to read the "real" political structure behind what he sees. Note that this view of reading is considered integral to the generative utility of Drag Queen Story Hour. The previously cited "Drag Pedagogy" paper, closes with these ominous sentences about their methodology:

> We're dressing up, we're shaking our hips, and we're finding our light—even in the fluorescents. We're reading books while we read each other's looks, and we're leaving a trail of glitter that won't ever come out of the carpet.

In fact, the authors devote an entire section of the paper to "Reading the Room: Inviting Strategic Defiance" in which the presence of the drag queen is meant to be generative to discussions on rulebreaking and gender-bending—a deliberate means of "strategic defiance" against norms of behavior and presentation (both literal and "queering"). This patently inappropriate destruction of boundaries is presented as a form of "reading" the allegedly inherently political nature of rules, norms, and expectations and how they might limit people and the ways they live their lives. They also devote an entire section to "alternate modes of kinship," which is later described as being "family friendly" in the sense of being "queer code" for one's so-called queer "family" on the street. How this mode of learning to "read" is understood as anything but deliberate and transparent grooming is a testament to the power of the "generative themes" method and "codification" to disguise the true, evil intentions and purposes of a hijacked education.

Of course, this is the kind of "reading" that a Freirean literacy program teaches in place of *actual reading*. What follows is what Freire calls the key stage in the (political) decodification process: "problematizing." It gets applied to whatever (oppression) has now been made visible to the learner through "reading" the codified presentation *as indicative of a structural-power phenomenon.* ("Aren't rules boring and burdensome? The other adults, like your parents, just don't want you to be like them...," the drag serpent whispers to a hypothetical kindergartner we'll call Eve.) Where codification is the preparation and reading is the initiation, problematizing is straight Marxism.

> In the practice that we defend, generative words—people's words—
> are used in realistic problem situations ("codifications") as challenges
> that call for answers from the illiterate learners. "To problematize"
> the word that comes from people means to problematize the the-
> matic element to which it refers. This necessarily involves an analysis
> of reality. And reality reveals itself when we go beyond purely sen-
> sible knowledge to the reasons behind the factors. Illiterate learners
> gradually begin to appreciate that, as human beings, to speak is not
> the same as to "utter a word." (*The Politics of Education*, p. 13)

This "reality" and "the reasons behind the factors" obviously refer to a Marxist analysis of the circumstance presented in the codification. "This change of perception, which occurs in the 'problematizing' of a reality in conflict, in viewing our problems in life in their true context, requires us to reconfront our reality" (p. 40), writes Freire. In other words, then, *problematization* is actually a process of bringing a Marxist analysis to bear on the codified situation. The learner in this stage is taught to critique the highlighted injustices and any alleged power dynamics producing them as structural phenomena, which is the intended meaning of "critical" in play—Marx's "ruthless criticism of all that exists." It is not the *critical thinking* it poses as in order to be deemed acceptable to administrators who implement it.

Lest there be any confusion, these two "critical" approaches are completely distinct, and the Critical Pedagogues are intentionally playing on an equivocation of the single word "critical." This fact is plainly visible in an explanation given in great clarity by another education Theorist, Alison Bailey. (Pardon the long quotation, but it is clarifying in the extreme.)

> Philosophers of education have long made the distinction between critical thinking and critical pedagogy. Both literatures appeal to the value of being "critical" in the sense that instructors should cultivate in students a more cautious approach to accepting common beliefs at face value. Both traditions share the concern that learners generally lack the ability to spot inaccurate, misleading, incomplete, or blatantly false claims. They also share a sense that learning a particular set of critical skills has a corrective, humanizing, and liberatory effect. The traditions, however, part ways over their definition of "critical." ... The critical-thinking tradition is concerned primarily with epistemic adequacy. To be critical is to show good judgment in recognizing when arguments are faulty, assertions lack evidence, truth claims appeal to unreliable sources, or concepts are sloppily crafted and applied. For critical thinkers, the problem is that people fail to "examine the assumptions, commitments, and logic of daily life... the basic problem is irrational, illogical, and unexamined living." In this tradition sloppy claims can be identified and fixed by learning to apply the tools of formal and informal logic correctly.
>
> Critical pedagogy begins from a different set of assumptions rooted in the neo-Marxian literature on critical theory commonly associated with the Frankfurt School. Here, the critical learner is someone who is empowered and motivated to seek justice and emancipation. Critical pedagogy regards the claims that students make in response to social-justice issues not as propositions to be assessed for their truth value, but as expressions of power that function to re-inscribe and perpetuate social inequalities. Its mission is to teach students ways of identifying and mapping how power shapes our understandings of the world. This is the first step toward resisting and transforming social injustices. By interrogating the politics of

knowledge-production, this tradition also calls into question the uses of the accepted critical-thinking toolkit to determine epistemic adequacy. To extend Audre Lorde's classic metaphor, the tools of the critical-thinking tradition (for example, validity, soundness, conceptual clarity) cannot dismantle the master's house: they can temporarily beat the master at his own game, but they can never bring about any enduring structural change. They fail because the critical thinker's toolkit is commonly invoked in particular settings, at particular times to reassert power: those adept with the tools often use them to restore an order that assures their comfort. They can be habitually invoked to defend our epistemic home terrains. ("Tracking Privilege-Preserving Epistemic Pushback in Feminist and Critical Race Philosophy Classrooms," *Hypatia* 32(4): 2017, pp. 881–882)

Of course, the method Freire repeatedly refers to as "the method we defend" *is exactly this Critical Pedagogy*. Freirean schools (which your kids probably attend) not only do not prioritize teaching critical thinking skills; they also see critical thinking skills as part of an overarching program of marginalizing other ways of knowing (namely, Marxism) and maintaining dominance for certain privileged groups. This is *precisely* the assumption around which Freire Marxified education, so we can understand that the "other ways of knowing" on the table are precisely those "facilitated" *into* learners by the Freirean codification and decodification method. As discussed in the generative themes chapter, this makes clear what the "decolonize the curriculum" program truly refers to in its emphasis on "other ways of knowing": replacing existing curriculum and curricular materials with materials that present or engender Freirean codification for a Marxified educational program of thought reform.

Again, in the modern classroom, this reading and problematizing process can be quite subtle or rather overt. In the subtler aspects of the problematizing process, students will be asked how the characters in the relevant stories must *feel* to be in those situations, say slavery or segregation, and then have those circumstances tied to alleged self-preserving social structures. They'll be led, or groomed, to see the "problematics" with whatever situation is present and to connect those to unjust power dynamics the critical educator is grooming them to see in virtually every circumstance as a matter of generating "political literacy," say "racial literacy" or "cultural competence" in more current parlance. This emphasis on feelings in this approach is also rooted in Freire: "During a discussion of a problematical situation—like codification—educators should ask peasants to write down their reactions—a simple phrase or whatever-first on the blackboard, and then, on a sheet of paper" (*The Politics of Education*, p. 24). In this case, those feelings will be attached to "whiteness" and "white supremacy," which will then be decodified through a doctrine of systemic racism that should succeed in raising a modicum of racial critical consciousness in the Critical Race Theory–groomed student "learner."

We thus see yet another connection to Freirean pedagogy in the current applications of Social-Emotional Learning, which is geared particularly to facilitate this process. Nowhere is this more true than with the current dominant strain, the overtly Marxist "Transformative SEL," promoted, for example, by CASEL (Collaborative for Academic, Social, and Emotional Learning). The SEL lesson will ask kids to identify how the people in the codification feel about the injustices under auspices of developing "social awareness," for example. In more overt cases, students will critique—or be given the critiques for—what is wrong in the situation in harsh, uncompromising terms about the racism, sexism, or other injustices that construct what is presented in the codified course materials.

Finally, once the abstracted codification has been "read" through Marxist political literacy (unjust structural power) and met its negative through problematization, the Freirean educator's role is to finish "decodifying" the codification, which is to say that he will connect it to the lived experience or "lived realities" of the learners. This *concretizes* the brainwashing. "The aim of decodification is to arrive at the critical level of knowing, beginning with the learner's experience of the situation in the 'real context.'" (*The Politics of Education*, p. 52). Freire is unambiguous on what this means: "While participating with the educator in 'decodifying' a codification, peasants analyze their reality and in their discourse they express levels of seeing themselves relative to an objective situation" (p. 24). The message in decodification is "it is *you* who was presented in this codification, which you now understand to be very problematic (on Marxist terms)." This, Freire tells us, makes the political context (oppression or complicity in oppressing) "concrete" for the learner and is a key step in his core pedagogical goal of raising a critical (Marxist) consciousness in the learner and calling it true "literacy."

In practice, the message given to children is frequently, "People who looked like you did *x* or had *y* done to them because that's how society is really organized." This part of the process involves the most "grooming" of the learner by the educator (facilitator) because it leads them to understand *themselves* in terms of the political conception of the educator. The objective of this part of the process is to awaken the critical consciousness that leads the learner to see themselves as part of the broad oppressor/oppressed structural dynamic of society and to realize their role in the objective of changing the society to end that dynamic entirely. That is, it is for raising an explicitly Marxist consciousness of whichever power structure the educator is making relevant at the time, whether race, sex, gender, sexuality, class, or something else.

The result of the concretization phase is that the Marxist analysis presented through the previous steps takes on a sense of reality and personalization. Freire claims this will spur learners to want to learn even more because of the relevance and importance of the injustice of the "concrete realities" of their situation. In fact, it does not. Instead, it achieves what Freire actually repeatedly says it must achieve and what he insists is the point of doing it in the first place: conscious praxis. What conscious praxis means, though, is becoming a Marxist activist. Learning is replaced with programming and political activation, in other words, exactly like we see in Providence, Rhode Island.

The Freirean Brainwashing Process

The codification and decodification approach is therefore a way to start with a generative concept and lead students in a grooming fashion through a deliberate process of political awakening—including to the need for class/group solidarity and social activism (to become "change agents"). It is a deliberate attempt to use tools like (Tranformative) Social-Emotional Learning, cultural competence, and Culturally Relevant Teaching to raise a critical (Identity Marxist) consciousness in students, often while sacrificing learning the underlying subject matter due to the misplaced pedagogical goals and commitments. That each of these domains explicitly says in modern academic writing about their purposes that among their goals is raising a critical consciousness in students, and that this means getting them to analyze not the course contents in academic terms but instead to study the power and power dynamics located within them, this is not only not a stretch but a simple statement of unobscured fact about their purpose.

In practice today, Transformative Social-Emotional Learning is almost certainly at the center of this process of connecting the feelings evoked through the earlier stages of the method to the learners themselves. That is, it is unambiguously Freirean pedagogy, which is to say Marxist thought reform. In *The Handbook of Social and Emotional Learning: Research and Practice* (2015), influential education activist Linda Darling-Hammond says this is the case *explicitly*. She writes, "this endeavor [SEL] includes the humanization of school institutions," which she explains thusly,

> As Paulo Freire explained, humanization is "the process of becoming more fully human as social, historical, thinking, communicating, transformative, creative persons who participate in and with the world." Educators, he argued, must "listen to their students and build on their knowledge and experiences in order to engage in ... personalized educational approaches that further the goals of humanization and transformation." Indeed, this is what we see in schools that successfully undertake the journey of becoming socially and emotionally educative. (*Handbook of Social and Emotional Learning*, p. xii)

The purpose of going through this process of conscientization is, again, to teach the learners to denounce the existing world while announcing the potentiality of a new world. This is believed only to be possible from a conscientized position. The codification/decodification process trains the learner to do this while also leading him into thought reform that helps him to be "reborn on the side of the oppressed" (adopt the "people's standpoint"). First, learners stand aside from the context of their lives so they can be critical of it. Then they read and problematize it (denunciation). If done from critical consciousness, thus "correctly" to the oppressed standpoint, it simultaneously announces a new possible arrangement for the world—specifically one in which that "problematic" is seen as bad and shunned (more detail is almost never available). Thus brainwashed, learners realize the power of their words and learn to "speak the word to proclaim the world" by denouncing what is and implicitly announcing what could possibly be.

VIII.

THE DIALOGICAL MODEL AND THE EGALITARIAN CLASSROOM

The final component of the Freirean model of education is perhaps the most famous: his so-called "dialogical model" of education. Appealing back to Plato and Socrates while saying they did it wrong because they didn't use it to raise critical consciousness, Freire insists that true and proper education must be "dialogical," which is to say that it is achieved through *dialogue* between "educators and learners *as equals.*" This is part of why Freire (sometimes) insists on the linguistic shift away from "teachers" and "students" to "educators" and "learners." As noted previously, the role of the "educator" is largely one of a *facilitator,* but this "dialogical" relationship should also consider learners as valid knowers in their own right. (Note: This framing mostly comes from *The Politics of Education*; in his earlier and more famous *Pedagogy of the Oppressed*, Freire merely hyphenates to indicate a new dialectically combined concept: "teacher-students" and "student-teachers.")

There is a deep Marxist theoretical explanation for this shift that can be summarized in shortest form by saying Freire believes the hierarchical relationship (in knowledge, power, etc.) between teachers and students reproduces a power dynamic that "domesticates" students and makes them the *objects* of an educational process rather than learning *subjects.* There are teachers who are assumed to be knowers and students who are assumed not to be knowers separated by the stratification of society around a structural power dynamic generated by what it means "to know." As a result, this hierarchical model is designed so that the teacher teaches established knowledge to the student, who is expected to learn it. All forms of education except Freire's "liberatory" approach are believed by Critical Pedagogues to *reproduce* this dynamic and thus maintain the evil intrinsically oppressive society. Since the teacher or administrators in the existing system gets to set the curriculum, they will do so in a disingenuous way that benefits them by maintaining the system as it is. Telling the student that it will further their career prospects and improve their lives is an ideological mystification of the education process, according to Freire, because it is only true within the system upheld by the ideological assumptions upon which society operates.

Freirean Pedagogy Implies a Concept of Man and the World

Freire wants to obliterate that system. He therefore bases his alternative approach on the underlying Marxist belief that man is ultimately his own creator and comes to know that through (1) realizing his own subjective consciousness, (2) realizing it can imagine something it wants to create in the world, (3) can make that thing as an object in the world, and (4) see himself, as creator, in the object he created from his subjective perspective. For Freire, following Marx, not only things but also society, other people, and man himself are the objects of this subject-object relationship that begins by realizing oneself to be a knowing and creative subject. "Every educational practice implies a concept of man and the world," Quoting him again to reorient ourselves, Freire writes,

> Experience teaches us not to assume that the obvious is clearly understood. So it is with the truism with which we begin: All educational practice implies a theoretical stance on the educator's part. This stance in turn implies—sometimes more, sometimes less explicitly—an interpretation of man and the world. It could not be

otherwise. The process of men's orientation in the world involves not just the association of sense images, as for animals. It involves, above all, thought-language, that is, the possibility of the act of knowing through his praxis, by which man transforms reality. For man, this process of orientation in the world can be understood neither as a purely subjective event, nor as an objective or mechanistic one, but only as an event in which subjectivity and objectivity are united. Orientation in the world, so understood, places the question of the purposes of action at the level of critical perception of reality.

If, for animals, orientation in the world means adaptation to the world, for man it means humanizing the world by transforming it. For animals there is no historical sense, no options or values in their orientation in the world; for man there is both an historical and a value dimension. Men have the sense of "project," in contrast to the instinctive routines of animals. (*The Politics of Education*, pp. 43–44)

As Freire sees it, it is only possible to engage this process fully in education if the "educators" and "learners" are in "authentic" dialogue "as equals" about the "real" conditions of their lives, by which is meant the Marxist interpretation of them, as we have discussed at length above. Through this dialogue, the "learners" can impart their "knowledge" of the conditions of their lives to the "educators," who will then use that information to identify generative themes ("cultural responsiveness") that can be presented back to the "learner" in codified form so that the conscientization process can take place.

Note, then, that the dialogical approach is not a stage of the Freirean educational program. It's a method that pervades all of its stages. In the first stage, dialogue is used as one of the tools to datamine students to discover their generative themes (while gaining their trust). It is then what is taken up by both educator and learner *together* in the decodification stage. Recall from the previous chapter that

Freire said the codification is abstract to both the educator and the learner who seek to discover its true meaning together in dialogue. Decodification—reading, problematizing, and ultimately identifying with and conscientizing—is a process done through dialogue, notably dialogue about the political context being presented in the guise of some other academic lesson. If the process actually proceeded to learning the relevant academic material, that, too, would be done "dialogically" and "as equals" in Freire's mind.

A Dialogue About Straw

Now, there's nothing here that automatically makes the dialogical approach to education necessarily and intrinsically worse than a lecture-based approach or other approaches. That's an empirical and contextual question that, in a responsible setting, could be investigated. Where Freire goes badly wrong, besides in what he misuses the approach to accomplish, is in asserting that all other approaches are terrible essentially for Marxist reasons. Therefore, while the dialogical approach might or might not have value or merit in some or many educational contexts, Freire doesn't admit this question. Other approaches are all "domesticating" models that fail in their agenda to educate the student genuinely.

Specifically, to get this dialogical method off the ground, Freire mischaracterizes traditional pedagogical approaches in two ways, one of which is his own invention: the "banking model," which is his, and the "nutritionist model," which he borrows from existentialist philosopher (and Marxist) Jean-Paul Sartre. These are essentially the same strawman of educational theory and practice. They are much more insidious than they sound. Both operate, says Freire, from the educator's underlying belief that the student is "empty" and needs to be filled or nourished with knowledge in order to become a knower, rather than being considered a knower in his own right by default—through recognizing his knowledges (mostly of his lived experiences[19]) and his "ways of knowing" as equally valid, if not superior, to "formal educational" knowledge and rigorous epistemology. Here, being a "knower" must be understood as a proxy for being "allowed to be" or being fully "human," as meant by Karl Marx, per Freire's Marxification of education.

> This "nutritionist" concept of knowledge, so common in current educational practice, is found very clearly in [forms of education where curricula are imposed]. Illiterates are considered "undernourished," not in the literal sense in which many of them really are, but because they lack the "bread of the spirit." Consistent with the concept of knowledge as food, illiteracy is conceived of as a "poison herb," intoxicating and debilitating persons who cannot read or write. Thus, much is said about the "eradication" of illiteracy to cure the disease. In this way, deprived of their character as linguistic signs constitutive of man's thought-language, words are transformed into mere "deposits of vocabulary"—the bread of the spirit that the illiterates are to "eat" and "digest." (*The Politics of Education*, p. 45)

In the "banking model" of education, which is essentially the same, Freire claims that educators and pedagogues, thus also students, see the uneducated or illiterate like empty bank deposit boxes to be filled with a kind of knowledge-based capital by the teacher.

> Narration (with the teacher as narrator) leads the students to memorize mechanically the narrated content. Worse yet, it turns them into "containers," into "receptacles" to be "filled" by the teacher. The more completely she fills the receptacles, the better a teacher

---

19   It's worth noting, at least in a footnote that's well-placed here, that Freire's Ph.D. is in phenomenology.

she is. The more meekly the receptacles permit themselves to be filled, the better students they are.

Education thus becomes an act of depositing, in which the students are the depositories and the teacher is the depositor. Instead of communicating, the teacher issues communiqués and makes deposits which the students patiently receive, memorize, and repeat. This is the "banking" concept of education, in which the scope of action allowed to the students extends only as far as receiving, filing, and storing the deposits. They do, it is true, have the opportunity to become collectors or cataloguers of the things they store. But in the last analysis, it is the people themselves who are filed away through the lack of creativity, transformation, and knowledge in this (at best) misguided system. For apart from inquiry, apart from the praxis, individuals cannot be truly human. Knowledge emerges only through invention and re-invention, through the restless, impatient, continuing, hopeful inquiry human beings pursue in the world, with the world, and with each other. (*Pedagogy of the Oppressed*, pp. 71–72)

For Freire, a "banking model" education—meaning *any* approach to education that isn't dialogical on Freirean terms—*robs people of what makes them truly human*, which is recognizing themselves as knowers who can use their (political) knowledge to transform the world. It also cannot do the real necessary work of education, which is to conscientize learners to become Marxist activists to transform the world in exactly this way.

To change the world through work, to "proclaim" the world, to express it, and to express oneself are the unique qualities of human beings. Education at any level will be more rewarding if it stimulates the development of this radical, human need for expression.

This is exactly what "banking education" (as I sometimes call it) does not do. In banking education an educator replaces self-expression with a "deposit" that a student is expected to "capitalize." The more efficiently he does this, the better educated he is considered. (*The Politics of Education*, p. 21)

It is important to understand Freire claims that teachers using any method outside of his think this way about their students and the purpose of education: they know something; the students don't; and it is their job to deposit knowledge into their empty bank accounts. From *Pedagogy of the Oppressed*, "In the banking concept of education, knowledge is a gift bestowed by those who consider themselves knowledgeable upon those whom they consider to know nothing" (p. 72). The students, in turn, are then expected, according to Freire, to "capitalize" upon these deposits by becoming productive members of the economic and social system that values "formal education" and sees it as necessary for its own (bourgeois) maintenance. As a result, when educating someone fails to produce elite success for them, the privileged can claim that it is somehow the fault of the learner, not the teacher, the system, or the allegedly bogus things it considers knowledge. The failed learner can be accused of being lazy, stupid, or otherwise deficient—giving birth to another term common in today's Freirean education programs, the *deficit model*, which explains student failures in terms of certain deficits, such as a stable home life or neighborhood condition. The "nutritionist model" of education is roughly the same thing replacing the analogy to bank deposits with food and drink to nourish someone into being a fully capable member of society (which Freire sees as bad, recall, because it leads to the reproduction and false legitimacy of the existing system).

The "banking model" of education is, of course, a Marxian strawman of education in a similar way that Marx's idea of "capitalism" is a strawman of market economies within political republics—with one important difference. The key difference is that while Marx merely strawmanned market economies, Freire is actually strawmanning an earlier collectivist educational misstep: the Prussian model of education ("school"), which Communists and progressives had eagerly exported (with their own spin) throughout the world. In other words, when Freire accuses the prevailing modes of education of being "domesticating" and implying that they indoctrinate rather than truly educate, he's not wholly wrong but misses the crucial point. In so doing, as a Gnostic Marxist, he then is able to use this earlier collectivist failure to insist that all methods of education *but his* somehow fail in the same way. The "banking model" of education is the name for this distortion, which Freire successfully used to characterize every form of education that might actually teach students anything.

Knowing Nothing, Together

In opposition to this fertile strawman, Freire proposes his "dialogical model." This concept is so central to Freire's educational program that he devotes two of the four chapters of *Pedagogy of the Oppressed* to detailing it. Still, as with many topics and points, he is far clearer in *The Politics of Education*:

> It might seem as if some of our statements defend the principle that, whatever the level of the learners, they ought to reconstruct the process of human knowing in absolute terms. In fact, when we consider adult literacy learning or education in general as an act of knowing, we are advocating a synthesis between the educator's maximally systematized knowing and the learners' minimally systematized knowing—a synthesis achieved in dialogue. The educator's role is to propose problems about the codified existential situations in order to help the learners arrive at a more and more critical view of their reality. The educator's responsibility as conceived by this philosophy is thus greater in every way than that of his colleague whose duty is to transmit information that the learners memorize. Such an educator can simply repeat what he has read, and often

misunderstood, since education for him does not mean an act of knowing.

The first type of educator, on the contrary, is a knowing subject, face to face with other knowing subjects. He can never be a mere memorizer, but a person constantly readjusting his knowledge who calls forth knowledge from his students. For him, education is a pedagogy of knowing. The educator whose approach is mere memorization is antidialogical; his act of transmitting knowledge is inalterable. For the educator who experiences the act of knowing together with his students, in contrast, dialogue is the sign of the act of knowing. He is aware, however, that not all dialogue is in itself the mark of a relationship of true knowledge. (*The Politics of Education*, pp. 54–55)

To Freire, then, only a teacher who engages in authentic dialogue with his students counts as a genuine "educator." He can't merely cover the curriculum because there's an excellent chance he doesn't even understand that he's just repeating the ideological mystification of society as though it constitutes education. The point of education has to be *critical*, as in Critical Theory, and that's only possible "dialogically." Otherwise, all that's occurring is a transfer of information that is, at best, hollow and meaningless, and, at worst, a vehicle for reproducing and maintaining an oppressive system. Doing this requires breaking down the hierarchy between teachers and students, as previously discussed.

Liberating education consists in acts of cognition, not transferals of information. It is a learning situation in which the cognizable object (far from being the end of the cognitive act) intermediates the cognitive actors—teacher on the one hand and students on the other. Accordingly, the practice of problem-posing education entails at the outset that the teacher-student contradiction to be resolved.

> Dialogical relations—indispensable to the capacity of cognitive actors to cooperate in perceiving the same cognizable object—are otherwise impossible. (*Pedagogy of the Oppressed*, pp. 79–80)

Without educating this way—his way—says Freire, the teacher will end up asserting authority rather than running a "democratic" classroom in which all are learners together. This will lead the teacher into the "banking model" of education, which will in turn not only oppress the students directly but will also lead them to preserve the existing culture and what it considers knowledge—rather than becoming a revolutionary pursuing Marxist liberation and humanization.

> The banking concept (with its tendency to dichotomize everything) distinguishes two stages in the action of the educator. During the first, he cognizes a cognizable object while he prepares his lessons in his study or his laboratory; during the second, he expounds to his students about that object. The students are not called upon to know, but to memorize the contents narrated by the teacher. Nor do the students practice any act of cognition, since the object towards which that act should be directed is the property of the teacher rather than a medium evoking the critical reflection of both teacher and students. Hence in the name of the "preservation of culture and knowledge" we have a system which achieves neither true knowledge nor true culture. (*Pedagogy of the Oppressed*, p. 80)

In place of this, Freire recommends his dialogical model, which he insists overcomes the "contradiction" of teacher and student by reorienting them as "educator" and "learners" who are "equally knowing subjects." The role of the "educator" as a facilitator into conscientization is then clarified, and their role will be to "unveil reality" as Marxists interpret it. The role of the learner is to engage in this process largely in a way that provides the generative themes and concepts that will be used to tailor the thought-reform program of the "educator" specifically to the context of the students' lives.

Becoming Collectivists, Together

This feature of the Freirean educational model makes complete sense of the data-mining surveys presented through Transformative Social-Emotional Learning programs. These provide the baseline by which the Marxist educator can create a perfectly suited thought-reform program in a, say, "culturally relevant" way.

> The adult literacy process as an act of knowing implies the existence of two interrelated contexts. One is the context of authentic dialogue between learners and educators as equally knowing subjects. This is what schools should be—the theoretical context of dialogue. The second is the real, concrete context of facts, the social reality in which men exist.
>
> In the theoretical context of dialogue, the facts presented by the real or concrete context are critically analyzed. This analysis involves the exercise of abstraction, through which, by means of representations of concrete reality, we seek knowledge of that reality. The instrument for this abstraction in our methodology is codification, or representation of the existential situations of the learners. (*The Politics of Education*, p. 51)

For Freire, no other form of education can possibly work than through what he views as "authentic dialogue," wherein "learners" are data-mined (by more or less sophisticated methods) to generate contexts and themes to produce codifications to be groomed into Marxist thought about the conditions of their own lives through further dialogue ("courageous conversations," perhaps, or otherwise what the Chinese Communists called "struggle"). All other approaches to education are meaningless, at best.

To be an act of knowing, the adult literacy process demands among teachers and students a relationship of authentic dialogue. True dialogue unites subjects together in the cognition of a knowable object, which mediates between them. If learning to read and write is to constitute an act of knowing, the learners must assume from the beginning the role of creative subjects.

It is not a matter of memorizing and repeating given syllables, words, and phrases, but rather of reflecting critically on the process of reading and writing itself, and on the profound significance of language. (*The Politics of Education*, pp. 49–50)

The dialogical model begins from an assumption that learners are already knowers who would be recognized as such if the existing power dynamic and "Messianic" model of traditional education would just see them for what they are. The knowledges they possess and ways of knowing (folk epistemologies) they employ are at least equally valid to those utilized by "formal education" and researchers. In fact, they are likely to be *more valid* by virtue of the underlying Marxist belief that the oppressed subject understands oppression and, once awakened to a Marxist consciousness, the nature of the oppressive society *better* than those who are privileged by it, if not uniquely.

Freire does not mince words about the purpose of his method. He openly says the point of dialogical education is to be—or become—revolutionary. In fact, he says it over and over again in *Pedagogy of the Oppressed*, directly and not just through references to "liberatory education" or "education for freedom," which mean the same thing. In fact, he says that the purpose of the dialogical approach is to establish and perpetuate "cultural revolution" and to seize power for his neo-Marxist movement:

For all the above reasons, I interpret the revolutionary process as dialogical cultural action which is prolonged in "cultural revolution" once power is taken. In both stages a serious and profound effort at *conscientização*—by means of which the people, through a true praxis, leave behind the status of *objects* to assume the status of historical *Subjects*—is necessary. (*Pedagogy of the Oppressed*, p. 160)

As you can see, the Marxist emphasis on becoming a "historical *Subject*," italicized and capitalized by Freire, and thus to de-objectify oneself, is the purpose of the dialogical method. The purpose isn't to become a mere conscious individual, however, but a member of his Communist collectivist vision for achieving utopia.

Since it is always a process, knowing presumes a dialectical situation: not strictly an "I think," but a "we think." It is not the "I think" that constitutes the "we think," but rather the "we think" that makes it possible for me to think. (*The Politics of Education*, pp. 99–100)

He puts this thoroughly collectivist (and fundamentally Marxist) idea even more strangely, and far less clearly, in *Pedagogy of the Oppressed*:

In the dialogical theory of action, Subjects meet in cooperation in order to transform the world. The antidialogical, dominating *I* transforms the dominated, conquered *thou* into a mere *it*. The dialogical *I*, however, knows that it is precisely the *thou* ("not-*I*") which has called forth his or her own existence. He also knows that the *thou* which calls forth his own existence in turn constitutes an *I* which has in his *I* its *thou*. The *I* and the *thou* thus become, in the dialectic of these relationships, two *thous* which become two *Is*. (p. 167)

I dare say this "dialectical" process of creating a "dialogical" hivemind of we-thinkers with your children, facilitated by Marxist groomers (and drag queens) posing as "educators," is not what you entrust and/ or pay schools to do, but because virtually all of our schools are Paulo

Freire's schools, that's what you're getting. In practice, this looks like the "educator" engaging in open dialogue with the "learners" about the relevant conditions of their life and designing, shall we say, a culturally relevant and responsive approach to teaching (the generative concepts approach). Based upon this student-led and educator-facilitated dialogue, generative concepts can be identified and amplified and the codification, problematization, decodification method can be devised in a "contextual way" to teach "political literacy" "as a process of change." The educator's role is to facilitate this discussion so that it always veers toward awakening critical consciousness and inspiring activism on its behalf. In the modern parlance, this is rendered as teaching students to become "change agents," often in "democratic" or "student-led" classrooms.

As a last note, another curious fad in education—project-based learning, usually student-led—also has its roots in this peculiar Freirean model. Freire suggested using "problem-posing" education, which isn't quite the same, strictly speaking, because the "problems" Freire meant to pose are generative political issues. In practice, though, "project-based learning" is often framed exactly this way, getting students to take on social, political, or environmental projects, which serve exactly this Freirean function. Freire describes the necessitity of this approach to his own model in *Pedagogy of the Oppressed*:

> Those truly committed to liberation must reject the banking concept in its entirety, adopting instead a concept of women and men as conscious beings, and consciousness as consciousness intent upon the world. They must abandon the educational goal of deposit-making and replace it with the posing of the problems of human beings in their relations with the world. "Problem-posing" education, responding to the essence of consciousness—*intentionality*—rejects communiqués and embodies communication. It epitomizes the special characteristic of consciousness: being *conscious of*, not

only as intent on objects but as turned in upon itself in a Jasperian "split"—consciousness as consciousness *of* consciousness. (p. 79)

Again, I would venture to guess that this is not what you expect out of your child's school or the "innovative" programs it implements, but because your kids go to Paulo Freire's schools, it's what you're getting—like it or not.

One may be tempted to offer a bone of fairness to Freire here since I keep invoking "your kids" in terms of the impacts of his work upon them and their (failing) educations. That is, Paulo Freire was working with adult peasants in South America—not children with adult teachers—when he introduced the idea that educators and learners should engage with one another *as equals*. Whatever Freire's intentions, then, this only makes the adoption of his work in North American Pre-K–12 education even more egregious. Simply put, adults and children emphatically *are not* equals, and it is professionally and developmentally inappropriate to engage in relationships as though they are. This fact is completely true even outside of the adoption of Queer Theory into Critical Pedagogy, which makes full use of many of the Freirean methods discussed throughout this guidebook. Positioning adult educators and child teachers as equals of a sort destroys a crucial boundary of authority and easily lends itself to an antagonistic relationship between the school and parents, where teachers and students, "as equals," are on a team together against parents, who are authority figures. As we saw, however, Freirean pedagogy targets any hierarchy of authority as a specific contributor to the problem defining society.

Queer Theory cannot be ignored on this front, either. It *openly* articulates its hostility to the concepts of childhood innocence and developmental appropriateness, and engaging in adult-child relationships (say, with drag queens) on these topics (in a Freirean way) *as equals* is not only ideological grooming on topics related to sex and sexuality but also a wide-open door to the darkest understandings of what the word "grooming" represents. It also willfully tends toward establishing parents as the problem and teachers as facilitators of and collaborators in (queer) children's liberation from them and their oppression. To quote from the "Drag Pedagogy" paper yet again:

> In a broader context, fostering collective unruliness also helps children to understand that they can have a hand in changing their environment. For any child who has ever asked a parent or teacher "why?" and been unsatisfied with the answer, "because I told you so," drag may help elucidate the arbitrariness of rules. By encouraging students to explore the boundaries of acceptability, drag offers a model for participating in a learning experience where axioms are meant to be challenged and authority is not a given. In the school environment, of course, oppressive conditions are often produced by the institution itself, and many children who intuitively resist these conditions are punished.
>
> DQSH performers demonstrate a refusal to be told what to do. In their demonstration of strategic defiance, drag storytellers engage in a more finely tuned kind of resistance that many children practice all the time. This embodied pedagogy teaches that, in unjust situations, people can use strategic tactics to push back against harmful actions. Drag may be especially well-positioned as a form of cultural production that, to paraphrase the writer and filmmaker Toni Cade Bambara, serves to "make revolution irresistible."

If I might be blunt, I cordially invite any decent person to try to convince me the people engaging in providing this "learning experience" don't belong in prison for what they're willfully and intentionally doing with children.

IX.

CONCLUSION

Our kids currently go to Paulo Freire's schools. These schools are unambiguously Marxist (unless we split hairs and call them neo-Marxist or Woke Marxist) in their architecture, pedagogy, methods, and goals. They have abandoned the idea of educating American children to grow toward becoming successful and prosperous adults in American society because they want to undermine, destroy, and replace American society. Rather than teaching literacy, numeracy, or other educational basics, Freirean schools use subject matter like reading, writing, mathematics, history, social studies, and science lessons to teach Marxist consciousness of one or more forms at a time. As a result of more than a decade of this practice, American schoolchildren are almost universally failing in basic competency in virtually every subject at virtually every grade level. They are more "politically literate," in the Freirean sense, than ever before, though. There's no other way to put this than that their education has been *stolen* from them and what replaces it is meant to be weaponized against the society upon which their futures depend.

In my opinion, even with every other significant and concerning problem happening in the country today, correcting the problem of Freirean education is a high-priority item, certainly within the top five biggest and most pressing issues, if it's not firmly in the top three. Freirean education is Marxist education, and it has no place in any American public school system. It is also explicitly religious education, for those who have read Freire and understand just how prominently Liberation Theology (fusion of Marxist Theory and Catholic theology) features not just in Freire's underlying thought but in his explicit framing of education. This, rightly understood, makes its inclusion in the American public school systems a severe First Amendment violation on multiple counts that, so far, goes unrecognized and uncorrected. Because it steals our children's educations from them, it also denies their legally protected right to obtain an education, which is a further potentially actionable violation against them still. Beyond these points, Freirean education is also a *failing education*.

Freirean education doesn't work, and, once seen for what it is, it is easy to understand why it doesn't work. It doesn't work *because it cannot work*, if "working" in education means *educating students*. It explicitly and intentionally replaces gaining mastery in any subject with using that subject as a proxy for generating "political literacy," by which is meant Marxist critical consciousness for engendering a cultural revolution, i.e., Maoist thought reform. Saying this requires absolutely no interpretation on my part but merely a straightforward repetition of Freire's exact words in their intended context. This is wholly inappropriate, completely ineffective at educating students, and a gross violation of the public's and parents' trust in these school systems and the teachers and administrators who facilitate their programs. There are also good reasons to believe it is blatantly illegal.

Parents send their children to public schools to be *educated*, not to be groomed into "political literacy" through a Marxist perversion of education. Taxpayers pay their property and other taxes to fund public schools because an *educated* populace is a public good in a democratic republic such as ours, whereas a know-nothing, discontented activist class of "emotional wrecks" committed to achieving utopian dreams through cultural revolution against the republic emphatically is *not* (as was demonstrated amply through the last half of 2020 throughout much of this country). Failing to teach our children to succeed, thrive, and prosper in the existing system because Freirean cultists working as "educators" hate the existing system betrays the public's and parents' trust, violates our children's basic rights, and has no place in any public school system in the United States of America or any other country that wants to stay healthy and intact in the long run.

Freire's *The Politics of Education* was published in 1985 and launched the relevance of Freirean education in North America. That means we are just shy of 40 years late to the project of removing Freirean influence from education, including especially colleges of education, which should have known better than to have ever taken it up. These colleges and their faculties and administrators have therefore betrayed us and our trust and have continued to do so with increasing fervor for four decades. Those responsible for this must be held accountable, and if it can be contrived, restitution to the generations they have already intentionally damaged is almost certainly owed, though it cannot possibly be repaid.

Simply, it is at the very least unquestionably already the second-best time to purge Freirean thought and methods from education at every level, Pre-K through Ph.D. It is my hope that this guide has helped expose Freirean education for what it is and for what it has done to our education system, children, and society. It is my further hope that it spurs productive action to remove as much of the Freirean influence from education as possible. It's not too late, but it's long past time.

X.

THE SHORT, SHORT, *SHORT* VERSION

Parts of this book are admittedly complex. It is also twice as long as I had intended it to be. Therefore, as a short appendix, I am including a lightly edited executive summary of the key points provided to a legal firm attempting to fight Marxist brainwashing in real American schools.

The Freirean approach to education is based off the work of the Brazilian Marxist Paulo Freire, who is most famous for his 1970 book *Pedagogy of the Oppressed*. This book is the third most-cited source in all of the social sciences and humanities and enjoys pride of place and curricular centrality in virtually every college of education in North America. The Freirean method, called "Critical Pedagogy" because it makes a Critical Theory (Neo-Marxist Theory) out of education itself, lies beneath, behind, or relevant to virtually every pedagogical trend in education over the last 20 to 30 years, including Social-Emotional Learning (SEL), Culturally Relevant Teaching, Comprehensive Sexuality Education, and project-based learning schemes. Culturally Relevant Teaching is unambiguously and unapologetically a direct repackaging of the Freirean approach into the context of "cultural competence" and American identity politics. Freire's pedagogy is a disaster for education and our children and has no place in our schools.

What Freire did, in short, was to "Marxify" education and knowing. That is, he created a Marxist Theory in which being educated, literate, or considered someone who knows (thus also what is designated as knowledge) operates in perfect parallel to the "bourgeois" class scapegoated by Karl Marx. Those who are considered uneducated, illiterate, or ignorant represent a lower class that can be made "class conscious" of their circumstances so that they will seek to initiate and complete a cultural revolution that moves them from the margins of society to its center, from which they can transform it. True education, for Freire, is a process of gaining "political literacy" through a process he describes as "conscientization," the gaining of critical (that is, Marxist) consciousness with activist commitments. Freire positions all genuine education as an imposition of the existing social and political order onto students so they will be "domesticated" by it and learn to reproduce and maintain it.

It should be noted that this process strongly resembles the "thought reform" (a.k.a. "brainwashing") technique used in Communist Chinese re-education prisons and schools in structure, method, and goals (see Lifton, R. J., *Thought Reform and the Psychology of Totalism: A Study of "Brainwashing" in China*). In that process, prisoners and students were presented with aspects of their own lives in which they were alleged to have committed crimes or otherwise failed to show solidarity with the Chinese people and its ("perfect") government, enhanced through regular interrogation. They were then put through long, abusive dialogue sessions (literally called "struggle") to help them learn to "recognize their crimes" so that they might "confess to them." Crimes are "recognized" when the prisoners learned to adopt "the people's standpoint" (i.e., once they are conscientized to the Chinese Marxist way of thought).

In our system, (Transformative) Social-Emotional Learning most directly mirrors the thought-reform process. It proceeds by presenting socially political and emotionally provocative material to children after surveying them to discover relevance. It then trains students to have the "correct" social attitudes and emotional responses to these stimuli posing as curriculum, especially to see them through an "inclusive" lens—or, as a pedagogy of the oppressed. Transformative SEL is unapologetic in stating its purpose is to raise a "critical consciousness," i.e., to induce Freirean conscientization through similar, though updated, methods.

The Freirean method can be summarized as following four distinct steps.

1. Identification of "generative themes"—In this step, dialogue, surveys, and provocations are used with students to identify words, concepts, and themes that have political relevance in their real lives. That is, it is a practice of data-mining students to find political sore spots relevant to their lives. Freire insists that this method take place between "educators and learners *as equals*," and the purpose is to identify politically, socially, and emotionally relevant ideas that can be used to encourage conscientization of the political context of their lives. Obviously, given the goal, these themes are usually negative and pick at points of potential political grievance that have been data-mined out of the students.

2. Presentation of the generative themes in "codified" form—In this step, the contents of the generative themes are fed back to the students in an "abstract" or "codified" form. Freire recommends picture form, since he was teaching literacy and couldn't expect his students to read. In the American education system, this might take the form of reading materials, vocabulary lists, contoured subject-matter lessons (like history through the 1619 Project and math through "ethnomathematics"), and special presentations—even the now-infamous "Drag Queen Story Hour" program refers to the purpose of the introduction of drag queens into schools as a "generative" method for "queer politics." The goal of this

step is to spur dialogue about the politically sensitive topics after presenting them in a way that might facilitate the goal of conscientization.

3. Marxist analysis of the codified themes, called "decodification"—In this step, the codifications from the previous step are "problematized," which means subjected to Marxist analysis in a dialogical format between learners and educators (acting as facilitators), and then made personal to the students. This process is done in a way that always tends toward conscientizing the students, which is to say teaching them to interpret their circumstances through a Marxist perspective, to apply them to their own lives, *and* to become activists to change those circumstances. In an experimental study of the Freirean adult-literacy method in Nigeria, by the end of this stage, students were reported to be "emotional wrecks" who only wanted to be activists and had no interest in learning to read.

4. Academic instruction through the aforementioned structure—Freire insists that the high level of engagement produced by the method will result in students using the generative themes (or words) as a basis for wanting to learn the subject matter and doing so thoroughly. Experiments, e.g., the one from Nigeria just mentioned, do not bear this hypothesis out. Freire insists that they will both learn the relevant academic material *and* become politically conscious (Marxist). In truth, only the second of these aims—the ignoble and destructive one—seems to be achieved by his method.

Again, the Freirean method of "education" is not an educational method at all. It is a means for politically grooming the perspective of students into a Marxist mindset, including to become activists. It is not only Marxist programming but an abject failure in all respects and has no place in American schools.

BIBLIOGRAPHY

Bailey, Alison. (2017) "Tracking Privilege-Preserving Epistemic Pushback in Feminist and Critical Race Philosophy Classes." *Hypatia* 32(4): 876–892.

Boler, Megan. (1999) *Feeling Power: Emotions and Education.* New York: Routledge.

Darling-Hammong, Linda. (2015) "Foreword—Social and Emotional Learning: Critical Skills for Building Healthy Schools," in *The Handbook of Social and Emotional Learning: Research and Practice*, eds. Joseph A. Durlak, Celene E. Domitrovich, Roger P. Weissberg, and Thomas P. Gullotta. New York: Guilford Press.

Freire, Paulo. (2005 [1970/1968]) *Pedagogy of the Oppressed.* 30th Anniversary Edition, Myra Berman Ramos, *trans.* New York: Continuum.

———. (1985) *The Politics of Education: Culture, Power, and Liberation.* Donaldo Macedo, *trans.* New York: Bergin & Garvey.

Gottesman, Isaac. (2016) *The Critical Turn in Education: From Marxist Critique to Poststructuralist Feminism to Critical Theories of Race.* Michael W. Apple, *ed.* New York: Routledge.

Keenan, Harper, and Lil Miss Hot Mess. (2021) "Drag pedagogy: The playful practice of queer imagination in early childhood." *Curriculum Inquiry* 50(5): 440–461.

Kobabe, Maia. (2019) *Gender Queer: A Memoir.* Oni Press.

Ladson-Billings, Gloria. (1995) "But That's Just Good Teaching! The Case for Culturally Relevant Pedagogy." *Theory into Practice* 34(3): 159–165.

———. (1995) "Toward a Theory of Culturally Relevant Pedagogy." *American Educational Research Journal* 32(3): 465–491.

Ladson-Billings, Gloria, and William Tate, IV. (1995) "Toward a Critical Race Theory of Education." *Teachers College Record* 97(1): 47–68.

Lifton, Robert Jay, M.D. (1989 [1961]) *Thought Reform and the Psychology of Totalism: A Study of "Brainwashing" in China.* Chapel Hill: University of North Carolina Press.

Lindsay, James. (2022) *Race Marxism: The Truth About Critical Race Theory and Praxis.* Orlando: New Discourses.

Livingston, Susannah E. (2022) "The Politics of Liberation and Love in Privileged Classrooms." *Rethinking Critical Pedagogy* 3(1): 1–35.

Lukács, György. (1967 [1923]) *History and Class Consciousness: Studies in Marxist Dialectics.* Rodney Livingstone, *trans.* Cambridge, MA: MIT Press.

Marcuse, Herbert. (1969) *An Essay on Liberation.* Boston: Beacon Press.

———. (1972) *Counter-revolution and Revolt.* Boston: Beacon Press.

Marx, Karl. (1977 [1959]) *Economic and Philosophic Manuscripts of 1844.* Moscow: Progress Publishers. Accessed at https://www.marxists.org/archive/marx/works/1844/epm/epm.pdf

Marx, Karl, and Friedrich Engels. *The Manifesto of the Party and Its Genesis.* Published by the Marxists Internet Archive. https://www.marxists.org/admin/books/manifesto/Manifesto.pdf

Ojokheta, K. O. (2007) "Paulo Freire's Literacy Teaching Methodology: Application and Implications of the Methodology in Basic Literacy Classes in Ibadan, Oyo State, Nigeria." Education for Everyone. Worldwide. Lifelong. / Adult Education and Development / Editions / AED 69/2007. Accessed online at https://www.dvv-international.de/en/adult-education-and-development/editions/aed-692007/10th-anniversary-of-paulo-freirersquos-death/paulo-freirersquos-literacy-teaching-methodology.

Pluckrose, Helen, and James Lindsay. (2020) *Cynical Theories: How Activist Scholars Made Everything About Race, Gender, and Identity—and Why This Harms Everybody.* Durham, NC: Pitchstone Press.